DYLAN FOX

Golang Programming For Beginners

Copyright © 2024 by Dylan Fox

All rights reserved. No part of this publication may be reproduced, stored or transmitted in any form or by any means, electronic, mechanical, photocopying, recording, scanning, or otherwise without written permission from the publisher. It is illegal to copy this book, post it to a website, or distribute it by any other means without permission.

First edition

This book was professionally typeset on Reedsy.
Find out more at reedsy.com

Contents

Introduction	1
Chapter 1: Getting Started with Go	8
Chapter 2: Go Language Fundamentals	16
Chapter 3: Control Structures	24
Chapter 4: Functions in Go	35
Chapter 5: Understanding Pointers	43
Chapter 6: Working with Structs and Methods	49
Chapter 7: Error Handling in Go	58
Chapter 8: Concurrency in Go	67
Chapter 9: Packages and Modules	77
Chapter 10: File Handling and I/O	85
Chapter 11: Testing and Benchmarking in Go	95
Chapter 12: Go with Web Development	102
Chapter 13: Working with Databases	112
Chapter 14: Error Logging and Debugging	122
Chapter 15: Deployment and Best Practices	132
Chapter 16: Go in the Cloud	142
Chapter 17: Conclusion	151

Introduction

Welcome to *Golang Programming for Beginners*! This book is designed to introduce you to the fundamentals of Go, one of the most popular programming languages today. Whether you're new to programming or an experienced developer looking to expand your skills, Go provides a modern, efficient, and easy-to-learn platform for creating fast and reliable software.

Throughout this book, we'll guide you through the essential concepts of Go, breaking down complex topics into manageable steps. You'll start by setting up your environment, writing your first Go program, and exploring the core principles that make Go unique. By the end of the book, you'll be equipped to build your own applications and have a solid understanding of Go's practical uses in real-world development.

Why Learn Go?

Go, also known as Golang, is a language that stands out for its simplicity, performance, and scalability. Developed by Google in 2007, Go was created to solve problems that traditional programming languages struggled with—primarily dealing with large-scale, cloud-based systems. Here's why Go is worth learning:

1. **Simplicity and Clarity**

2. Go was intentionally designed with simplicity in mind. Its syntax is minimal, making it easier to read and write code compared to other modern programming languages. This simplicity reduces the learning curve and helps prevent unnecessary complexity, making your code easier to maintain.
3. **Performance**
4. Go compiles directly to machine code, which means it can achieve near C-like performance without the complexity of managing memory manually. This makes Go an excellent choice for building high-performance applications, such as web servers or cloud-based systems, where speed is critical.
5. **Concurrency Support**
6. Go was built with concurrency at its core. Goroutines, Go's lightweight thread management system, make it incredibly easy to write programs that can handle multiple tasks simultaneously, making Go ideal for large-scale distributed systems.
7. **Strong Community and Ecosystem**
8. Go has an active, growing community of developers and a wide range of third-party libraries and tools. This strong ecosystem ensures that as a Go developer, you'll have access to numerous resources, from tutorials and forums to reusable libraries that make development easier.
9. **Used by Top Tech Companies**
10. Go is trusted by companies like Google, Uber, Dropbox, and Docker for mission-critical software. Learning Go can open up opportunities in industries where performance and scalability are essential.

In short, Go's balance of simplicity, performance, and concurrency makes it a powerful tool for any developer, particularly those interested in building fast, scalable systems.

INTRODUCTION

A Brief History of Go

Go was created by Robert Griesemer, Rob Pike, and Ken Thompson, three engineers at Google, in response to frustrations with the limitations of other languages, particularly in the context of large-scale system development. The development began in 2007, and Go was released as an open-source project in 2009.

At the time, Google was dealing with massive codebases written in languages like C++ and Java. These languages, while powerful, were cumbersome for managing large teams and complex systems. Go was designed to improve the development experience by offering:

- **Fast compilation times**, reducing the downtime developers face while waiting for code to compile.
- **Concurrency features** built directly into the language, making it easier to write programs that perform multiple tasks at once.
- **A simpler syntax**, making Go code easier to read and maintain, even for large teams.

Since its release, Go has grown rapidly in popularity, particularly in industries like cloud computing, DevOps, and microservices. Major platforms and tools, such as Kubernetes and Docker, were built using Go, cementing its reputation as the go-to language for cloud-native development.

What You'll Learn in This Book

This book is designed to take you from beginner to proficient Go programmer. Whether you're completely new to programming or have experience with other languages, the chapters will guide you through the key concepts in Go, providing hands-on examples and exercises along the way.

Here's what you can expect to learn:

- **Go Basics**: Understand the core syntax and structure of Go programs,

from variables and data types to control structures like loops and conditionals.
- **Functions and Methods**: Learn how to write reusable code with functions and how Go's unique approach to methods can help you manage complexity.
- **Concurrency**: Discover Go's built-in concurrency features like Goroutines and Channels, which make it easy to write programs that do multiple things at once.
- **Error Handling**: Master Go's idiomatic approach to handling errors and writing robust, crash-proof code.
- **Go for the Web**: Explore how Go can be used to build web applications and APIs, making it a great choice for backend development.
- **Working with Databases**: Learn how to integrate Go with databases like MySQL and PostgreSQL, and perform CRUD operations efficiently.
- **Testing and Benchmarking**: Go includes strong support for testing and performance benchmarking. You'll learn how to write tests, measure performance, and optimize your code.
- **Deploying Go Applications**: Finally, you'll see how to package and deploy your Go applications, whether on local servers or in the cloud.

By the end of this book, you'll be comfortable writing your own Go programs and applying what you've learned to real-world projects.

Setting Up Your Go Development Environment

Before diving into Go programming, you'll need to set up your development environment. Fortunately, Go is easy to install and configure on all major platforms, including Windows, macOS, and Linux.

Step 1: Download and Install Go

To start, visit the official Go website (https://golang.org/dl/) and download the appropriate installation package for your operating system. Follow the installation instructions for your platform:

- **Windows**: Run the installer and follow the prompts. Once installed, you may need to restart your terminal or command prompt to ensure Go is added to your system's PATH.
- **macOS**: Use the downloaded installer or install Go using a package manager like Homebrew (brew install go).
- **Linux**: Download the tarball from the official site, extract it, and move it to the /usr/local directory. Then, add Go to your PATH by updating your shell profile.

Step 2: Verify Installation

Once Go is installed, open a terminal or command prompt and type the following command to verify the installation:

```go
Copy code
go version
```

If Go is installed correctly, this will print the installed version of Go.

Step 3: Set Up Your Go Workspace

Go follows a specific directory structure known as the workspace. This workspace is where all your Go code will reside. To set up your Go workspace:

1. Create a directory where you want to store your Go projects. For example:

```bash
Copy code
mkdir $HOME/go
```

1. Set the GOPATH environment variable to point to this directory. In Unix-based systems, you can add this line to your .bashrc or .zshrc file:

```bash
Copy code
export GOPATH=$HOME/go
```

1. Add Go's bin directory to your PATH to ensure you can run compiled Go programs:

```bash
Copy code
export PATH=$PATH:$GOPATH/bin
```

Step 4: Test Your Go Installation

To make sure everything is working, create a simple Go program. Open your terminal and run the following commands to create a new Go project:

```bash
Copy code
mkdir -p $GOPATH/src/hello
cd $GOPATH/src/hello
```

Inside the hello directory, create a new file called main.go:

```css
Copy code
nano main.go
```

Add the following Go code:

```go
Copy code
```

INTRODUCTION

```
package main

import "fmt"

func main() {
    fmt.Println("Hello, World!")
}
```

Save the file and run the program using the following command:

```go
Copy code
go run main.go
```

You should see the output:

```
Copy code
Hello, World!
```

Congratulations! Your Go environment is now set up, and you're ready to begin your journey into Go programming.

Chapter 1: Getting Started with Go

In this chapter, we will guide you through the process of setting up Go on your system, writing your first Go program, understanding Go's workspace and package structure, and running and compiling your Go programs. By the end of this chapter, you'll be equipped to start coding in Go.

Installing Go on Windows, macOS, and Linux

Before you can start writing Go programs, you'll need to install the Go compiler and runtime. Here's a step-by-step guide for installing Go on the three major operating systems.

1. **Installing Go on Windows**
   - **Step 1:** Visit the official Go download page and download the Windows installer (.msi file).
   - **Step 2:** Run the installer and follow the prompts to complete the installation.
   - **Step 3:** During installation, the Go binary will automatically be added to your system's PATH. If not, you can add it manually. To verify, open Command Prompt and run:

```go
Copy code
go version
```

- If Go is installed correctly, you'll see the installed Go version.

2. Installing Go on macOS

- **Step 1:** Visit the official Go download page and download the macOS package.
- **Step 2:** Open the package and follow the installation instructions.
- **Step 3:** Alternatively, you can use Homebrew to install Go:

```go
Copy code
brew install go
```

- **Step 4:** After installation, open your terminal and verify the installation by typing:

```go
Copy code
go version
```

3. Installing Go on Linux

- **Step 1:** Download the Go binary tarball from the official Go download page.
- **Step 2:** Extract the tarball:

```bash
Copy code
tar -C /usr/local -xzf go1.x.x.linux-amd64.tar.gz
```

- **Step 3:** Add Go to your system's PATH by editing your .bashrc or .zshrc file:

```ruby
Copy code
export PATH=$PATH:/usr/local/go/bin
```

- **Step 4:** Verify your installation by typing:

```go
Copy code
go version
```

Now that Go is installed, you're ready to start coding!

Writing Your First Go Program: "Hello, World!"

Once Go is installed, it's time to write your first Go program. Let's create the classic "Hello, World!" program to familiarize ourselves with the Go syntax and structure.

1. **Create a new directory for your Go project**
2. In your terminal or command prompt, navigate to your workspace and create a directory called hello:

```bash
Copy code
mkdir $HOME/go/src/hello
cd $HOME/go/src/hello
```

1. **Create the Go file**
2. Inside the hello directory, create a new file called main.go. Open the file with a text editor of your choice (e.g., nano, VS Code):

```css
Copy code
nano main.go
```

1. **Write the code**
2. Add the following code to your main.go file:

```go
Copy code
package main

import "fmt"

func main() {
    fmt.Println("Hello, World!")
}
```

1. Let's break it down:

- package main: Declares this file as part of the main package. Every Go application must have a main package to run.

- import "fmt": Imports the fmt package, which provides formatted I/O functions.
- func main(): This is the entry point for the program, similar to main functions in other programming languages.
- fmt.Println("Hello, World!"): This function prints "Hello, World!" to the console.

1. **Run the program**
2. To execute your Go program, type the following command in your terminal:

```go
Copy code
go run main.go
```

1. You should see the output:

```
Copy code
Hello, World!
```

Understanding the Go Workspace and Package Structure

Go encourages a specific structure for your code, which revolves around the concept of workspaces and packages. Understanding this is crucial to effectively organizing your Go projects.

1. **Go Workspace**

The Go workspace is where all your Go code resides. A typical Go workspace contains three main directories:

- **src**: This is where your Go source files (the actual code) are located.
- **pkg**: This directory stores compiled package objects.

- **bin**: This contains the compiled binary executables for your Go programs.

By default, Go sets up your workspace in the $GOPATH, which is usually set to $HOME/go on Unix systems or C:/Users/YourName/go on Windows.

2. **Package Structure**

Go projects are organized into packages. Every Go source file belongs to a package, and packages provide a way to organize related code together.

- **Main Package**: Every Go program that you want to execute must contain a main package, which includes the main() function. This function serves as the entry point for your application.
- **Custom Packages**: You can also create your own reusable packages by placing code in different directories within the src folder and importing them in other Go files.

Example structure of a simple Go project:

```bash
Copy code
/go
    /src
        /myproject
            main.go
        /mypackage
            util.go
    /pkg
    /bin
```

Running and Compiling Go Programs

Once you've written a Go program, you have two main options: you can run it directly, or you can compile it into an executable binary.

1. **Running Go Programs**

Running Go programs without compiling is useful during development. Use the go run command, which compiles and runs your code in one step:

```go
Copy code
go run main.go
```

This command compiles the source code in memory and immediately runs the program.

2. Compiling Go Programs

When you're ready to deploy or distribute your program, you'll need to compile it into a binary. Go provides a simple way to do this using the go build command:

```go
Copy code
go build main.go
```

This will create a binary executable named main (or main.exe on Windows) in the current directory. You can now run the executable directly:

```bash
Copy code
./main    # On Unix-based systems
main.exe  # On Windows
```

3. Cross-Compilation

One of Go's powerful features is its ability to cross-compile programs for different operating systems and architectures. For example, you can compile a Go program for Linux on a Windows machine by setting the GOOS and GOARCH environment variables:

```go
Copy code
GOOS=linux GOARCH=amd64 go build main.go
```

This command generates a binary that can be run on a 64-bit Linux machine, regardless of where the program was compiled.

Chapter 2: Go Language Fundamentals

In this chapter, we will cover the fundamental elements of the Go programming language. Understanding these basics is crucial to writing efficient and effective Go programs. This chapter introduces you to the basic syntax and structure of Go programs, variables and constants, data types, operators and expressions, and the essential fmt package for handling input and output.

Basic Syntax and Structure of a Go Program

Go's syntax is simple and clean, making it relatively easy to understand, even if you're new to programming. Here's a breakdown of the main components of a Go program.

1. Package Declaration

Every Go source file begins with a package declaration. If you're writing an executable program, the package must be declared as main, which indicates that the file contains the main() function, the entry point of the application.

```go
Copy code
package main
```

2. Imports

Go uses the import keyword to bring in other packages. For example, the standard fmt package is used for formatted input and output. Import statements go immediately after the package declaration.

```go
Copy code
import "fmt"
```

3. The Main Function

In Go, the main() function is the entry point for your program. When you run a Go application, the code inside the main() function is executed first.

```go
Copy code
func main() {
    fmt.Println("Hello, World!")
}
```

4. Code Structure

- **Functions**: Functions in Go start with the func keyword, followed by the function name, parameters, and return types (if any).
- **Blocks**: Blocks of code are enclosed in curly braces {}.
- **No Semicolons**: Go statements don't end with semicolons; they're inferred automatically at the end of lines.

Here's a basic Go program structure:

```go
Copy code
package main

import "fmt"

func main() {
```

```
fmt.Println("This is a basic Go program")
}
```

Variables, Constants, and Data Types

Variables and constants are fundamental building blocks in Go. Let's explore how to declare and use them in Go programs.

1. Variables

Variables in Go are explicitly declared, and their types are inferred when necessary. Variables can be declared using the var keyword or with shorthand notation.

- **Variable Declaration with var:**

```go
Copy code
var name string = "John"
var age int = 30
```

- **Shorthand Variable Declaration:** You can declare variables without specifying the type using the shorthand :=, which allows Go to infer the type.

```go
Copy code
name := "John"
age := 30
```

- **Multiple Variable Declaration:** You can declare multiple variables in a single statement.

```go
Copy code
var x, y int = 1, 2
```

2. Constants

Constants are values that cannot be modified after they are declared. They are declared using the const keyword and must be assigned at the time of declaration.

```go
Copy code
const Pi = 3.14
```

3. Data Types

Go has a set of primitive data types:

- **Integers**: int, int8, int16, int32, int64
- **Unsigned Integers**: uint, uint8, uint16, uint32, uint64
- **Floating-Point Numbers**: float32, float64
- **Strings**: string
- **Booleans**: bool

Example of variable declarations with different data types:

```go
Copy code
var isTrue bool = true
var price float64 = 99.99
var message string = "Hello, Go!"
```

4. Type Conversion

Go does not support implicit type conversion. You must explicitly convert variables between types using built-in functions such as int(), float64(), etc.

```go
Copy code
var a int = 10
var b float64 = float64(a)
```

Operators and Expressions in Go

Go supports a range of operators for working with variables and data. These include arithmetic, comparison, logical, and bitwise operators.

1. **Arithmetic Operators**

Arithmetic operators are used to perform mathematical operations.

- + (Addition)
- - (Subtraction)
- * (Multiplication)
- / (Division)
- % (Modulus)

Example:

```go
Copy code
a := 10
b := 5
sum := a + b  // 15
diff := a - b // 5
```

2. **Comparison Operators**

Comparison operators compare two values and return a boolean result (true or false).

- == (Equal)
- != (Not equal)
- > (Greater than)
- < (Less than)

- >= (Greater than or equal to)
- <= (Less than or equal to)

Example:

```go
a := 10
b := 5
isEqual := (a == b)   // false
isGreater := (a > b)  // true
```

3. Logical Operators

Logical operators are used to combine multiple conditions.

- && (Logical AND)
- || (Logical OR)
- ! (Logical NOT)

Example:

```go
a := true
b := false
result := a && b   // false
```

4. Assignment Operators

Assignment operators are used to assign values to variables. You can also combine them with arithmetic operators.

- = (Assignment)
- +=, -=, *=, /=, %=

Example:

```go
Copy code
a := 10
a += 5  // a = 15
```

5. Bitwise Operators

Go also includes bitwise operators, which work on the binary representations of integers.

- & (AND)
- | (OR)
- ^ (XOR)
- « (Left shift)
- » (Right shift)

Input and Output in Go: fmt Package

Go's fmt package provides standard input and output functions that are used for displaying information and reading user input.

1. Printing Output

The most commonly used function in the fmt package is fmt.Println, which prints output followed by a new line.

```go
Copy code
fmt.Println("Hello, Go!")
```

- **Other Output Functions:**
- fmt.Print(): Prints output without adding a new line.
- fmt.Printf(): Prints formatted output using verbs (e.g., %s for strings, %d for integers).

Example:

```go
Copy code
name := "John"
age := 30
fmt.Printf("Name: %s, Age: %d\n", name, age)
```

2. Reading Input

You can also use the fmt.Scan() function to read user input.

```go
Copy code
var name string
fmt.Print("Enter your name: ")
fmt.Scan(&name)
fmt.Println("Hello, ", name)
```

- **Other Input Functions:**
- fmt.Scanf(): Reads formatted input.
- fmt.Scanln(): Reads input until a newline is encountered.

Example of formatted input:

```go
Copy code
var age int
fmt.Print("Enter your age: ")
fmt.Scanf("%d", &age)
fmt.Println("You are", age, "years old")
```

Chapter 3: Control Structures

Control structures are essential in any programming language as they allow you to control the flow of your programs. In this chapter, we will cover how Go handles conditional statements, looping constructs, and data structures like arrays, slices, and maps. Understanding these elements will help you create more dynamic and interactive programs.

Conditional Statements: if, else, switch

Conditional statements in Go are used to execute different code blocks based on certain conditions.

1. **if and else Statements**

The if statement is used to evaluate a condition and execute code if the condition is true. You can extend this behavior with else and else if to handle additional conditions.

- **Basic Syntax:**

```go
Copy code
if condition {
    // code to be executed if condition is true
} else if anotherCondition {
    // code to be executed if anotherCondition is true
```

CHAPTER 3: CONTROL STRUCTURES

```go
} else {
    // code to be executed if no conditions are true
}
```

- **Example:**

```go
Copy code
age := 18
if age >= 18 {
    fmt.Println("You are eligible to vote.")
} else {
    fmt.Println("You are not eligible to vote.")
}
```

- **Short Declaration in if Statements:** Go allows short variable declarations inside if statements, which can be useful for evaluating expressions without polluting the outer scope.

```go
Copy code
if value := 10; value > 5 {
    fmt.Println("Value is greater than 5")
}
```

2. switch Statements

switch statements in Go are a cleaner way to handle multiple conditions compared to if-else chains. They evaluate an expression and execute the matching case.

- **Basic Syntax:**

```
go
Copy code
switch expression {
case value1:
    // code block for value1
case value2:
    // code block for value2
default:
    // code block if no case matches
}
```

- **Example:**

```
go
Copy code
day := "Monday"
switch day {
case "Monday":
    fmt.Println("Start of the work week.")
case "Friday":
    fmt.Println("Almost weekend!")
default:
    fmt.Println("Midweek day.")
}
```

- **No Fallthrough by Default:** Unlike C-based languages, Go does not fall through to subsequent cases by default. To explicitly allow fallthrough, you use the fallthrough keyword.

```go
Copy code
switch num := 2; num {
case 1:
    fmt.Println("One")
case 2:
    fmt.Println("Two")
    fallthrough
case 3:
    fmt.Println("Three")
}
```

Looping Constructs: for, range, break, continue

Go provides a simple but powerful looping mechanism using for. Go does not have while or do-while loops; instead, everything can be done with the versatile for loop.

1. **for Loop**

The for loop in Go can be used in multiple forms, similar to traditional for, while, and infinite loops.

- **Basic Syntax:**

```go
Copy code
for initialization; condition; post {
    // code to execute
}
```

- **Example:**

```go
Copy code
```

```go
for i := 0; i < 5; i++ {
    fmt.Println(i)
}
```

- **Infinite Loop:** The for loop without a condition creates an infinite loop.

```go
Copy code
for {
    fmt.Println("Infinite Loop")
}
```

2. range Loop

The range keyword is used to iterate over collections like arrays, slices, maps, and strings.

- **Example with Slice:**

```go
Copy code
numbers := []int{10, 20, 30, 40}
for index, value := range numbers {
    fmt.Printf("Index: %d, Value: %d\n", index, value)
}
```

- **Ignoring Index or Value:** If you only need the value, you can ignore the index by using an underscore (_).

```go
Copy code
for _, value := range numbers {
    fmt.Println(value)
}
```

3. break and continue Statements

- **break**: Stops the loop before it has completed all iterations.

```go
Copy code
for i := 0; i < 10; i++ {
    if i == 5 {
        break
    }
    fmt.Println(i) // Will print numbers from 0 to 4
}
```

- **continue**: Skips the current iteration and moves to the next one.

```go
Copy code
for i := 0; i < 10; i++ {
    if i%2 == 0 {
        continue // Skip even numbers
    }
    fmt.Println(i) // Will print odd numbers from 1 to 9
}
```

Working with Arrays and Slices

Arrays and slices are key data structures in Go, often used to store collections of elements.

1. **Arrays**

An array is a fixed-size, sequential collection of elements of the same type.

- **Declaration and Initialization:**

```go
Copy code
var arr [5]int
  // Declare an array of 5 integers
arr[0] = 1
  // Set the first element to 1
numbers := [3]int{1, 2, 3}
// Shorter way to initialize an array
```

- **Accessing Elements:** You access elements by their index, starting from 0.

```go
Copy code
fmt.Println(numbers[1]) // Output: 2
```

2. **Slices**

Slices are a more flexible and powerful abstraction built on top of arrays. Unlike arrays, slices can grow or shrink in size.

- **Creating Slices:**

```go
Copy code
```

```go
slice := []int{1, 2, 3, 4, 5}
// Declare and initialize a slice
fmt.Println(slice)
   // Output: [1 2 3 4 5]
```

- **Using make() to Create Slices:** You can use the make() function to create a slice with a specified length and capacity.

```go
Copy code
slice := make([]int, 5)
// Creates a slice of length 5 with zero values
```

- **Slicing an Array or Slice:** You can create a new slice from an existing array or slice.

```go
Copy code
numbers := []int{1, 2, 3, 4, 5}
subSlice := numbers[1:4] // Creates a slice [2, 3, 4]
```

- **Appending Elements:** Use the append() function to add elements to a slice.

```go
Copy code
slice := []int{1, 2, 3}
slice = append(slice, 4, 5)
fmt.Println(slice) // Output: [1 2 3 4 5]
```

Introduction to Maps and Their Usage

Maps are Go's built-in data type used to associate keys with values, similar to dictionaries in Python or hash tables in other languages.

1. Creating Maps

Maps can be created using the make() function or by using a map literal.

- **Using make():**

```go
Copy code
myMap := make(map[string]int)
// Creates an empty map with string keys and int values
```

- **Map Literal:**

```go
Copy code
myMap := map[string]int{
    "Alice": 25,
    "Bob":   30,
}
```

2. Adding, Accessing, and Deleting Elements

- **Adding Elements:**

```go
Copy code
myMap["Charlie"] = 35
```

- **Accessing Elements:**

```go
Copy code
age := myMap["Alice"]
fmt.Println(age) // Output: 25
```

- **Checking for Key Existence:** To check if a key exists in the map, use the "comma ok" idiom.

```go
Copy code
value, ok := myMap["Bob"]
if ok {
    fmt.Println("Bob's age is", value)
} else {
    fmt.Println("Bob not found")
}
```

- **Deleting Elements:** Use the delete() function to remove key-value pairs from a map.

```go
Copy code
delete(myMap, "Alice")
```

3. Iterating Over Maps

You can use a for range loop to iterate over the keys and values in a map.

```go
Copy code
for key, value := range myMap {
    fmt.Printf("%s is %d years old\n", key, value)
}
```

Chapter 4: Functions in Go

Functions are the building blocks of any program and are essential to organizing code logically and efficiently. In this chapter, we will explore how to define and call functions in Go, use parameters and return values, leverage named return values and multiple returns, create anonymous functions and closures, and understand recursion. This will provide you with a solid understanding of how to use functions to write reusable and modular code.

Defining and Calling Functions

In Go, functions are defined using the func keyword, followed by the function name, parameters, and return type (if any). Functions help break down complex problems into smaller, reusable pieces of code.

1. **Basic Syntax**

The general syntax for defining a function in Go is:

```go
Copy code
func functionName(parameter1 type,
 parameter2 type) returnType {
    // Function body
}
```

2. **Example: A Simple Function**

The following function calculates the sum of two integers:

```go
Copy code
func add(a int, b int) int {
    return a + b
}
```

- **Function Name**: add is the name of the function.
- **Parameters**: a and b are the parameters, both of type int.
- **Return Type**: The function returns an int.

3. Calling a Function

You can call a function by using its name and passing the required arguments.

```go
Copy code
result := add(5, 3)
fmt.Println("Sum:", result)   // Output: Sum: 8
```

Function Parameters and Return Values

Functions can accept parameters and return values. Parameters allow you to pass values to a function, while return values allow the function to send data back to the caller.

1. Single Parameter and Return Value

A function can take a single parameter and return a single value.

```go
Copy code
func greet(name string) string {
    return "Hello, " + name
}
```

Usage:

```go
Copy code
message := greet("Alice")
fmt.Println(message)  // Output: Hello, Alice
```

2. Multiple Parameters

Functions can also accept multiple parameters.

```go
Copy code
func multiply(a int, b int) int {
    return a * b
}
```

Usage:

```go
Copy code
product := multiply(4, 5)
fmt.Println("Product:", product)
// Output: Product: 20
```

3. Multiple Return Values

Go functions can return multiple values, which is a feature that is not found in many other languages.

```go
Copy code
func divide(a int, b int) (int, int) {
    quotient := a / b
    remainder := a % b
    return quotient, remainder
}
```

Usage:

```go
Copy code
quotient, remainder := divide(10, 3)
fmt.Printf("Quotient: %d, Remainder: %d\n", quotient, remainder) // Output: Quotient: 3, Remainder: 1
```

Named Return Values and Multiple Returns

Go allows you to define names for return values in the function signature. This can make your code more readable and reduce the need for explicitly declaring variables in the function body.

1. **Named Return Values**

You can declare return values directly in the function signature, which allows you to use those variables directly in the function.

```go
Copy code
func rectangleProps(length, width float64) (area, perimeter float64) {
    area = length * width
    perimeter = 2 * (length + width)
    return // No need to specify variables explicitly since they are named
}
```

Usage:

```go
Copy code
area, perimeter := rectangleProps(5, 3)
fmt.Printf("Area: %.2f, Perimeter: %.2f\n", area, perimeter)
// Output: Area: 15.00, Perimeter: 16.00
```

2. **Multiple Return Values Use Case**

Multiple return values are commonly used for functions that need to return both a result and an error.

```go
Copy code
func safeDivide(a, b int) (int, error) {
    if b == 0 {
        return 0, fmt.Errorf ("cannot divide by zero")
    }
    return a / b, nil
}
```

Usage:

```go
Copy code
result, err := safeDivide(10, 0)
if err != nil {
    fmt.Println("Error:", err)
} else {
    fmt.Println("Result:", result)
}
```

Anonymous Functions and Closures

Anonymous functions and closures are powerful tools for writing concise and functional-style code in Go.

1. **Anonymous Functions**

Anonymous functions are functions without a name. They are often used as immediate expressions or passed as arguments to other functions.

- **Defining an Anonymous Function:**

```go
Copy code
```

```go
func() {
    fmt.Println("This is an anonymous function")
}()
```

- Here, the function is defined and immediately called.
- **Assigning to a Variable:** You can assign an anonymous function to a variable and call it later.

```go
Copy code
add := func(a int, b int) int {
    return a + b
}
result := add(3, 4)
fmt.Println("Result:", result)
// Output: Result: 7
```

2. Closures

A closure is an anonymous function that captures and retains access to the variables in the surrounding scope.

- **Example of Closure:**

```go
Copy code
func main() {
    increment := func() func() int {
        count := 0
        return func() int {
            count++
            return count
        }
```

```go
    }

    nextCount := increment()
    fmt.Println(nextCount()) // Output: 1
    fmt.Println(nextCount()) // Output: 2
    fmt.Println(nextCount()) // Output: 3
}
```

- In this example, nextCount retains access to the count variable, even after increment() has finished execution. This is what makes it a closure.

Recursion in Go

Recursion is a technique in which a function calls itself to solve smaller instances of the same problem. Recursion is especially useful for problems that can be broken down into subproblems of the same type, such as calculating factorials or solving the Fibonacci sequence.

1. **Factorial Example**

A classic example of recursion is calculating the factorial of a number.

go
Copy code
```go
func factorial(n int) int {
    if n == 0 {
        return 1
    }
    return n * factorial(n-1)
}
```

Usage:

go
Copy code
```go
fmt.Println("Factorial of 5:",
 factorial(5)) // Output: Factorial of 5: 120
```

2. Fibonacci Sequence Example

The Fibonacci sequence is another classic example of recursion.

```go
Copy code
func fibonacci(n int) int {
    if n <= 1 {
        return n
    }
    return fibonacci(n-1) + fibonacci(n-2)
}
```

Usage:

```go
Copy code
fmt.Println("Fibonacci of 6:", fibonacci(6))  // Output: Fibonacci of 6: 8
```

3. Understanding Recursion Depth

It's important to be cautious with recursion as it can lead to stack overflow errors if the base condition is not met or if the recursion depth is too high. Always ensure your recursive function has a well-defined base case that will eventually stop the recursion.

Chapter 5: Understanding Pointers

Pointers are a crucial concept in programming, providing powerful ways to directly access and manipulate memory. In Go, understanding pointers is key to writing efficient code, especially when dealing with large data structures or functions that modify their arguments. This chapter will cover what pointers are, how to create and use them, pointer dereferencing, and the difference between using pointers and values in function arguments.

What are Pointers?

Pointers are variables that store the memory address of another variable. Instead of holding a value directly, a pointer points to the location in memory where the value is stored.

1. **Why Use Pointers?**
- **Efficient Memory Usage**: When working with large data structures, passing them as pointers can save memory and increase performance, as only the address is passed, not the entire structure.
- **Modifying Values**: Pointers allow functions to modify variables in place, as they can directly access the memory address of the variable.

2. **Pointer Basics**

In Go, a pointer is represented by an asterisk (*) before the type it points to. For instance, *int is a pointer to an int.

- **Declaring a Pointer:**

```go
Copy code
var ptr *int
```

- **Zero Value of a Pointer:** The zero value of a pointer is nil, which means it doesn't point to anything.
- **Address Operator (&):** To get the address of a variable, use the address operator (&).

```go
Copy code
var x int = 10
ptr := &x  // ptr is a pointer to x
```

Creating and Using Pointers in Go

1. Creating a Pointer

To create a pointer, you first need a variable to point to, then use the address operator (&) to get its memory address.

- **Example:**

```go
Copy code
var number int = 42
var ptr *int = &number
fmt.Println(ptr)   // Output: Memory address of `number`
```

- **Short Declaration:** You can also use short declaration (:=) to create a pointer.

```go
Copy code
number := 42
ptr := &number
fmt.Println(ptr)   // Output: Memory address of `number`
```

2. Modifying Values via Pointers

You can modify the value of a variable by dereferencing its pointer. This allows you to change the original value stored at that memory address.

- **Example**:

```go
Copy code
number := 42
ptr := &number
*ptr = 100   // Changes the value of `number` to 100
fmt.Println(number)   // Output: 100
```

Pointer Dereferencing

Pointer dereferencing is the process of accessing or modifying the value at the memory address to which the pointer points. In Go, you use the asterisk (*) to dereference a pointer.

1. **Dereferencing a Pointer**

When you dereference a pointer, you access the value at the memory address stored in the pointer.

- **Example**:

```go
Copy code
number := 58
ptr := &number
fmt.Println(*ptr)   // Output: 58
```

- In this example, *ptr gives you the value of number. You can also modify the value directly through the pointer:

```go
Copy code
*ptr = 60
fmt.Println(number)   // Output: 60
```

2. Pointer vs. Normal Variable Access

- **Pointer**: Holds the memory address of a value.
- **Dereferenced Pointer** (*ptr): Accesses the actual value at the memory address.

Pointers vs. Values in Function Arguments

Understanding the difference between passing values and pointers to functions is crucial for efficient Go programming. By default, Go passes arguments by value, meaning that a copy of the data is passed into the function, and changes to the copy do not affect the original variable.

1. Pass by Value

When a variable is passed to a function by value, the function receives a copy, and any modifications made inside the function do not affect the original value.

- **Example**:

```go
Copy code
func incrementValue(num int) {
    num++
}

func main() {
    a := 5
    incrementValue(a)
    fmt.Println(a)   // Output: 5 (No change)
}
```

- In this case, incrementValue only increments the local copy of a.

2. Pass by Pointer (Pass by Reference)

Passing a pointer to a function allows the function to modify the original value, as the function works with the actual memory address of the variable.

- **Example**:

```go
Copy code
func incrementPointer(num *int) {
    *num++   // Dereferencing the pointer to increment the actual value
}

func main() {
    a := 5
    incrementPointer(&a)   // Passing the address of `a`
    fmt.Println(a)   // Output: 6 (Value is modified)
}
```

3. Use Cases for Pointers

- **Modify Data in a Function**: If you need a function to modify its argument, use a pointer.
- **Passing Large Data Structures**: Passing a pointer instead of a copy reduces memory usage and improves performance.
- **Example: Swapping Values**:

```go
Copy code
func swap(x, y *int) {
    temp := *x
    *x = *y
    *y = temp
}

func main() {
    a, b := 10, 20
    swap(&a, &b)
    fmt.Printf("a: %d, b: %d\n", a, b)   // Output: a: 20, b: 10
}
```

- In this example, the swap function uses pointers to modify the values of a and b directly.

Chapter 6: Working with Structs and Methods

Structs are one of the most important features of Go, allowing you to create custom data types that bundle related information together. Methods, on the other hand, allow you to define behaviors that are specific to these structs. Together, they help make Go a powerful tool for building reusable and modular code. In this chapter, we will cover defining structs, using structs with functions, methods to add behaviors, working with pointers to structs, and using composition as an alternative to inheritance.

Defining Structs: Custom Data Types in Go

A struct is a composite data type that groups multiple fields under a single name. It is ideal for representing more complex data than primitive types.

1. **Defining a Struct**

To define a struct, use the type keyword followed by the struct name and fields.

- **Basic Struct Syntax:**

```
go
Copy code
```

```go
type Person struct {
    Name string
    Age  int
}
```

- **Example Usage:**

```go
Copy code
func main() {
    p1 := Person{
        Name: "Alice",
        Age:  30,
    }
    fmt.Println("Name:", p1.Name, "Age:", p1.Age)
}
```

2. Creating Struct Instances

Struct instances can be created in several ways:

- **Direct Initialization:**

```go
Copy code
p1 := Person{"Alice", 30}
```

- **Field Names Initialization (Recommended for Clarity):**

```go
Copy code
p2 := Person{
    Name: "Bob",
    Age:  25,
}
```

- **Using new() to Create Pointers to Structs:**

```go
Copy code
p3 := new(Person)
p3.Name = "Charlie"
p3.Age = 40
```

3. Accessing Struct Fields

Struct fields are accessed using the dot operator (.).

```go
Copy code
fmt.Println(p1.Name)    // Output: Alice
p1.Age = 31             // Modify field value
```

Structs and Functions

Functions in Go can work with structs to perform operations on them. You can pass structs as arguments to functions, and return them as well.

1. Passing Structs to Functions

When a struct is passed to a function, it is passed by value, meaning a copy is made.

- **Example:**

```go
Copy code
func printPerson(p Person) {
    fmt.Printf("Name: %s, Age: %d\n", p.Name, p.Age)
}

func main() {
    p := Person{Name: "Alice", Age: 30}
    printPerson(p) // Output: Name: Alice, Age: 30
}
```

2. Modifying Struct Fields in Functions

To modify the fields of a struct inside a function, you need to pass a pointer to the struct.

- **Example:**

```go
Copy code
func updateAge(p *Person, newAge int) {
    p.Age = newAge
}

func main() {
    p := Person{Name: "Alice", Age: 30}
    updateAge(&p, 35)
    fmt.Println("Updated Age:", p.Age)
// Output: Updated Age: 35
}
```

Methods: Adding Behavior to Structs

Methods allow you to associate behaviors with a struct, similar to adding member functions to a class in object-oriented programming. In Go, methods are functions that have a receiver.

1. Defining Methods

A method is defined using the func keyword, followed by a receiver (the struct it is associated with), the method name, and parameters.

- **Example of a Method:**

```go
Copy code
type Person struct {
    Name string
    Age  int
}

// Method to print a greeting
func (p Person) greet() {
    fmt.Printf("Hello, my name is %s.\n", p.Name)
}

func main() {
    p := Person{Name: "Alice", Age: 30}
    p.greet()   // Output: Hello, my name is Alice.
}
```

2. **Pointer Receivers vs. Value Receivers**

- **Value Receivers**: When a method has a value receiver, the method works on a copy of the struct, meaning that any modifications made inside the method do not affect the original struct.
- **Pointer Receivers**: When a method has a pointer receiver, the method works directly on the original struct, allowing you to modify its fields.
- **Example with Pointer Receiver:**

```go
Copy code
```

```go
func (p *Person) incrementAge() {
    p.Age++
}

func main() {
    p := Person{Name: "Alice", Age: 30}
    p.incrementAge()
    fmt.Println("Age after increment:", p.Age) // Output: Age after increment: 31
}
```

Use pointer receivers if the method needs to modify the struct or if copying the struct would be too expensive in terms of memory.

Structs and Pointers

Working with pointers to structs helps in modifying struct fields and managing memory efficiently.

1. **Creating Struct Pointers**

Pointers to structs can be created using the & operator or the new() function.

- **Example:**

```go
Copy code
p := Person{Name: "Bob", Age: 40}
ptr := &p
fmt.Println(ptr.Name)   // Access fields using pointer (automatically dereferenced)
ptr.Age = 41            // Modify value through pointer
```

2. **Automatic Dereferencing**

Go simplifies working with struct pointers by automatically dereferencing them when accessing fields. You don't need to explicitly dereference pointers when accessing struct fields.

- **Example:**

```go
Copy code
p := &Person{Name: "Charlie", Age: 45}
fmt.Println(p.Name)  // Automatically dereferences to get `Name`
```

This feature makes it easier to work with pointers, without constantly needing to use the * operator.

Composition over Inheritance in Go

Go does not support traditional inheritance like in object-oriented languages, but it uses **composition** to achieve similar functionality. Instead of creating hierarchies of structs, Go encourages you to compose structs from smaller, reusable components.

1. **Embedding Structs**

Struct embedding is a way to include one struct inside another, allowing you to promote fields and methods from the embedded struct.

- **Example:**

```go
Copy code
type Address struct {
    City  string
    State string
}

type Person struct {
    Name    string
    Age     int
    Address // Embedding the Address struct
}

func main() {
```

```go
    p := Person{
        Name: "Alice",
        Age:  30,
        Address: Address{
            City:  "New York",
            State: "NY",
        },
    }
    fmt.Printf("%s lives in %s, %s\n", p.Name, p.City, p.State)
    // Output: Alice lives in New York, NY
}
```

- **Promoted Fields**: In the above example, City and State are promoted fields of Person. This means you can access City and State directly via the Person instance.

2. Method Promotion through Embedding

Methods defined on embedded structs are promoted to the embedding struct, allowing you to call those methods as if they were defined on the outer struct.

- **Example:**

```go
Copy code
type Contact struct {
    Email string
    Phone string
}

type Employee struct {
    Name    string
    Contact // Embedding Contact struct
}
```

```
func (c Contact) getContactInfo() {
    fmt.Printf("Email: %s, Phone: %s\n", c.Email, c.Phone)
}

func main() {
    e := Employee{
        Name: "John",
        Contact: Contact{
            Email: "john@example.com",
            Phone: "123-456-7890",
        },
    }
    e.getContactInfo()   // Output: Email: john@example.com, Phone: 123-456-7890
}
```

3. Advantages of Composition

- **Flexibility**: Struct composition allows you to reuse code without being restricted by rigid class hierarchies.
- **Promotes Reuse**: You can embed multiple structs in one, allowing for modular and reusable code.
- **Simplicity**: Composition is generally simpler and more straightforward than inheritance, as it avoids complex hierarchies and the issues that arise from them.

Chapter 7: Error Handling in Go

Error handling is a core concept in Go, and the language provides a robust yet simple way to manage errors. Unlike other languages that rely on exceptions, Go encourages explicit error handling, which results in more readable and predictable code. In this chapter, we will explore Go's philosophy of error handling, how to use the error type, create custom errors, and utilize panic, recover, and defer to manage critical failures.

The Philosophy of Error Handling in Go

Go's approach to error handling is different from many other programming languages. Instead of exceptions, Go uses explicit error returns. This makes error management explicit, predictable, and forces developers to think about error scenarios as they write code.

1. **No Exceptions, Only Errors**
   - Go treats errors as values that can be returned by functions, which makes handling them a conscious decision at each step.
   - Functions that may produce an error will usually return an additional value of type error.
   - **Example:**

```go
Copy code
func divide(a, b int) (int, error) {
    if b == 0 {
        return 0, fmt.Errorf("cannot divide by zero")
    }
    return a / b, nil
}

func main() {
    result, err := divide(10, 0)
    if err != nil {
        fmt.Println("Error:", err)
        return
    }
    fmt.Println("Result:", result)
}
```

2. Explicit Handling Encouraged

Go's explicit error handling improves program robustness, as developers are forced to handle every possible error scenario. This also makes code easier to understand, as error paths are not hidden in the flow of execution.

3. Idiomatic Error Checking

The common idiom for checking errors in Go is:

```go
Copy code
result, err := functionCall()
if err != nil {
    // handle error
}
```

This encourages developers to check for and handle errors immediately, preventing them from being ignored.

Using the Error Type

In Go, the error type is used to represent errors. The error type is a built-in interface with a single method:

```go
Copy code
type error interface {
    Error() string
}
```

This means any type that implements the Error() method can be used as an error. Go provides a predefined way to create and return errors using the errors.New() function from the errors package or fmt.Errorf() for formatted errors.

1. **Returning Errors**

- **Using errors.New():**

```go
Copy code
import "errors"

func getAge(name string) (int, error) {
    if name == "" {
        return 0, errors.New("name cannot be empty")
    }
    return 25, nil
}
```

- **Using fmt.Errorf():** fmt.Errorf() provides formatted error messages, which can be helpful when more details need to be added.

```go
Copy code
```

```go
import "fmt"

func getDetails(id int) (string, error) {
    if id <= 0 {
        return "", fmt.Errorf("invalid ID: %d", id)
    }
    return "Details", nil
}
```

2. Example of Handling Errors

```go
Copy code
func main() {
    _, err := getDetails(-1)
    if err != nil {
        fmt.Println("Error:", err)
    } else {
        fmt.Println("Operation succeeded")
    }
}
```

Custom Errors with error.New() and fmt.Errorf()

Creating custom errors in Go allows you to provide more context to the issues your program might encounter. The errors package and fmt.Errorf() function are commonly used to create descriptive error messages.

1. **Creating Custom Errors with errors.New()**

The errors.New() function allows you to create simple error messages.

- **Example:**

```go
Copy code
import "errors"
```

```go
var ErrInvalidAge = errors.New("age cannot be negative")

func validateAge(age int) error {
    if age < 0 {
        return ErrInvalidAge
    }
    return nil
}
```

2. Using fmt.Errorf() for Formatting

The fmt.Errorf() function is useful for creating detailed, formatted error messages.

- **Example:**

```go
Copy code
func validateSalary(salary int) error {
    if salary < 0 {
        return fmt.Errorf("invalid salary: %d", salary)
    }
    return nil
}

func main() {
    err := validateSalary(-100)
    if err != nil {
        fmt.Println("Error:", err)
    }
}
```

3. Wrapping Errors (Go 1.13 and Later)

Go 1.13 introduced error wrapping using fmt.Errorf() and %w to provide more context to existing errors.

- **Example:**

CHAPTER 7: ERROR HANDLING IN GO

```go
import "fmt"

func readFile(filename string) error {
    if filename == "" {
        return fmt.Errorf("failed to open file: %w",
        errors.New("filename cannot be empty"))
    }
    return nil
}
```

You can use errors.Is() and errors.As() to unwrap and inspect wrapped errors.

Panic, Recover, and Defer

Go uses panic to indicate that something went wrong at a very low level, typically errors from which the program cannot recover. recover is used to regain control of a program after a panic. Finally, defer allows for delayed function execution, often used for cleanup.

1. **Panic**

panic stops the execution of a program, but defer statements are still executed.

- **Example of panic:**

```go
func divide(a, b int) int {
    if b == 0 {
        panic("division by zero")
    }
    return a / b
}

func main() {
```

```go
    fmt.Println("Starting program")
    divide(10, 0) // This will cause a panic
    fmt.Println("This will not be printed")
}
```

Use panic sparingly; it is typically used for unrecoverable errors such as out-of-bounds array accesses or critical issues.

2. Recover

recover is used to catch a panic and prevent it from crashing the program. It is used inside a deferred function.

- **Example of recover:**

```go
Copy code
func safeDivide(a, b int) {
    defer func() {
        if r := recover(); r != nil {
            fmt.Println("Recovered from panic:", r)
        }
    }()
    fmt.Println("Result:", divide(a, b))
}

func main() {
    safeDivide(10, 0)
    fmt.Println("Program continues after recovery")
}
```

In the example above, recover() prevents the program from terminating after a panic.

3. Defer

The defer keyword is used to ensure a function is executed after the current function completes, even if a panic occurs. defer is commonly used for cleanup operations like closing files or releasing resources.

- **Example of defer:**

```go
Copy code
func main() {
    defer fmt.Println("Deferred: This runs after main completes")
    fmt.Println("This runs first")
}
```

- **Output:**

```less
Copy code
This runs first
Deferred: This runs after main completes
```

4. **Using defer for Resource Management**

defer is often used to ensure that resources are properly released, such as closing files or database connections.

- **Example with File Handling:**

```go
Copy code
import (
    "fmt"
    "os"
)

func main() {
    file, err := os.Open("example.txt")
    if err != nil {
```

```
        fmt.Println("Error:", err)
        return
    }
    defer file.Close()  // Ensures the file is closed before exiting

    // Read and process the file
    fmt.Println("File opened successfully")
}
```

The defer statement ensures that file.Close() is called no matter what happens in the function, which helps manage resources effectively and prevent resource leaks.

Chapter 8: Concurrency in Go

Concurrency is one of Go's standout features, making it highly efficient for building scalable systems. Go's concurrency model is built around goroutines and channels, which makes managing concurrent tasks simple and safe. In this chapter, we will cover an introduction to goroutines, synchronization with WaitGroup, using channels for communication, understanding buffered vs. unbuffered channels, and leveraging select statements for handling multiple channel operations.

Introduction to Goroutines

A **goroutine** is a lightweight thread managed by the Go runtime. Goroutines are a powerful way to run multiple functions concurrently.

1. **Starting a Goroutine**

To start a goroutine, simply prepend the go keyword to a function call. This tells Go to execute the function concurrently.

- **Example:**

```
go
Copy code
func printHello() {
    fmt.Println("Hello, Goroutine!")
}
```

```
func main() {
    go printHello()
    fmt.Println("Main function")
}
```

- In this example, printHello() runs as a goroutine. The main function may complete before the goroutine has a chance to execute, which is why we often need synchronization techniques.

2. **Goroutines vs Threads**

- **Lightweight**: Goroutines are much lighter compared to system threads. You can easily run thousands of goroutines within a single Go program.
- **Efficient Scheduling**: The Go runtime has a scheduler that efficiently manages the execution of goroutines.

3. **Anonymous Functions as Goroutines**
Goroutines can also be started using anonymous functions.

```
go
Copy code
func main() {
    go func() {
        fmt.Println("Hello from an anonymous goroutine!")
    }()
    fmt.Println("Main function")
}
```

Synchronization with WaitGroups

When dealing with multiple goroutines, it's important to ensure that all of them complete their tasks before the program terminates. **WaitGroup** from the sync package is useful for managing such scenarios.

1. Using sync.WaitGroup

WaitGroup helps synchronize goroutines by waiting for a collection of them to finish.

- **Basic Syntax:**

```go
Copy code
import (
    "fmt"
    "sync"
)

func worker(id int, wg *sync.WaitGroup) {
    defer wg.Done() // Mark this goroutine as done when finished
    fmt.Printf("Worker %d starting\n", id)
    // Simulate some work
    fmt.Printf("Worker %d done\n", id)
}

func main() {
    var wg sync.WaitGroup
    for i := 1; i <= 3; i++ {
        wg.Add(1) // Add a new goroutine to the WaitGroup
        go worker(i, &wg)
    }
    wg.Wait() // Wait for all goroutines to complete
    fmt.Println("All workers completed")
}
```

- wg.Add(1): Adds a count for each goroutine that starts.
- wg.Done(): Decrements the counter when the goroutine completes.
- wg.Wait(): Blocks until the counter reaches zero.

Channels: Communicating Between Goroutines

Channels are Go's way of enabling communication between goroutines.

Channels provide a mechanism for goroutines to share data safely without explicit locking.

1. Creating Channels

Channels are created using the make() function.

- **Unbuffered Channel:**

```go
Copy code
ch := make(chan int)
```

2. Sending and Receiving Data

- **Sending Data to a Channel:**

```go
Copy code
ch <- 42   // Send value 42 to channel ch
```

- **Receiving Data from a Channel:**

```go
Copy code
value := <-ch  // Receive value from channel ch
```

3. Example of Channel Communication

```go
Copy code
func main() {
    ch := make(chan string)

    go func() {
        ch <- "Hello, Channel!" // Send a message to the channel
    }()

    message := <-ch   // Receive the message from the channel
    fmt.Println(message)   // Output: Hello, Channel!
}
```

In this example, one goroutine sends a message, while the main function waits to receive it.

4. Channel Directions

A channel can be restricted to only send or receive data in function signatures.

- **Send-Only Channel:**

```go
Copy code
func sendData(ch chan<- int) {
    ch <- 100
}
```

- **Receive-Only Channel:**

```go
Copy code
func receiveData(ch <-chan int) {
    value := <-ch
```

```
fmt.Println(value)
}
```

Buffered vs. Unbuffered Channels

Channels can be either **unbuffered** or **buffered**.

1. Unbuffered Channels

- **Blocking Behavior**: In unbuffered channels, both sending and receiving are blocking operations. The sender waits until there is a receiver, and the receiver waits until there is data.
- **Example**:

```go
Copy code
ch := make(chan int)    // Unbuffered channel
```

2. Buffered Channels

Buffered channels allow you to specify the number of values that can be stored in the channel. This makes sending non-blocking until the buffer is full.

- **Creating Buffered Channels:**

```go
Copy code
ch := make(chan int, 3)    // Buffered channel with capacity 3
```

- **Example:**

```go
Copy code
func main() {
    ch := make(chan int, 2)
    ch <- 1
    ch <- 2
    fmt.Println(<-ch)  // Output: 1
    fmt.Println(<-ch)  // Output: 2
}
```

- In this example, ch has a buffer of size 2, so it can hold up to two values before any receiver needs to take action.

3. **When to Use Buffered Channels**

Buffered channels are useful when you want to decouple the timing between sending and receiving, reducing the need for immediate hand-off between goroutines.

Select Statements and Channel Operations

Select is a control structure unique to Go that lets a goroutine wait on multiple channel operations. It is similar to switch, but for channels, allowing you to listen to multiple channels at once.

1. **Basic select Syntax**

select blocks until one of its cases can make progress.

- **Example:**

```go
Copy code
func main() {
    ch1 := make(chan string)
    ch2 := make(chan string)
```

```go
    go func() {
        ch1 <- "Message from channel 1"
    }()

    go func() {
        ch2 <- "Message from channel 2"
    }()

    select {
    case msg1 := <-ch1:
        fmt.Println(msg1)
    case msg2 := <-ch2:
        fmt.Println(msg2)
    }
}
```

- In this example, select waits until either ch1 or ch2 sends a value. Whichever sends first gets executed.

2. Handling Timeouts with select

select can also be used to implement timeouts using the time.After function.

- **Example:**

```go
Copy code
import (
    "fmt"
    "time"
)

func main() {
    ch := make(chan string)

    go func() {
```

```go
        time.Sleep(2 * time.Second)
        ch <- "Data from goroutine"
    }()

    select {
    case msg := <-ch:
        fmt.Println(msg)
    case <-time.After(1 * time.Second):
        fmt.Println("Timeout occurred")
    }
}
```

- Here, if the message is not received from the channel within 1 second, the timeout case executes.

3. **Default Case in select**

A default case in a select allows the select block to proceed immediately if no other channel operations are ready.

- **Example:**

```go
Copy code
func main() {
    ch := make(chan int, 1)
    ch <- 1

    select {
    case value := <-ch:
        fmt.Println("Received:", value)
    default:
        fmt.Println("No value ready")
    }
}
```

- If no channels are ready, the default case executes.

Chapter 9: Packages and Modules

Go's package and module system is essential for organizing your code and managing dependencies. Packages help in structuring code logically, while modules simplify dependency management. In this chapter, we will explore how to use built-in packages, create your own packages, understand Go modules, and manage dependencies effectively.

Using Built-in Packages

Go has a comprehensive standard library that contains numerous built-in packages. These packages provide a wide range of functionality, from basic I/O operations to complex cryptographic algorithms.

1. **Importing Built-in Packages**

To use a built-in package, you need to import it. Go's import keyword allows you to access functions, types, and other elements within a package.

- **Example: Using the fmt Package**

```go
Copy code
import "fmt"

func main() {
    fmt.Println("Hello, World!")
```

}

2. Popular Built-in Packages

- **fmt**: Provides formatted I/O functions (Println, Printf, etc.).
- **os**: Contains functions for dealing with the operating system (os.Open, os.Exit).
- **strings**: Includes utilities for working with strings (strings.Contains, strings.Split).
- **math**: Contains mathematical functions (math.Sqrt, math.Pow).
- **time**: Provides utilities for measuring and displaying time (time.Now, time.Sleep).

3. Example: Using the strings Package

```go
Copy code
import (
    "fmt"
    "strings"
)

func main() {
    input := "Golang is great"
    upper := strings.ToUpper(input)
    fmt.Println(upper)   // Output: GOLANG IS GREAT
}
```

Creating Your Own Packages

Packages in Go are designed to help organize your code logically. By creating your own packages, you can reuse code across multiple parts of your project or even share it with others.

1. Package Structure

Each package is a collection of Go source files that are located in the same directory. All files in a directory belong to the same package.

- **Example Package Directory Structure:**

```go
Copy code
/myproject
   /mathutils
      add.go
      subtract.go
   main.go
```

2. Defining a Custom Package

Create a new directory for your package (e.g., mathutils). Inside this directory, create Go files with functions that can be shared.

- **add.go in mathutils Package:**

```go
Copy code
package mathutils

func Add(a, b int) int {
    return a + b
}
```

3. Using Your Custom Package

To use a custom package, you need to import it in your main program. Go treats the directory name as the package name by default.

- **Example: Using the mathutils Package in main.go**

```go
Copy code
package main

import (
    "fmt"
    "myproject/mathutils"
)

func main() {
    sum := mathutils.Add(5, 3)
    fmt.Println("Sum:", sum)    // Output: Sum: 8
}
```

4. Exporting and Unexporting

- Functions or variables that start with an uppercase letter (e.g., Add) are **exported** and can be accessed from other packages.
- Functions or variables that start with a lowercase letter (e.g., subtract) are **unexported** and can only be accessed within the same package.

Understanding Go Modules

Modules are a way to manage and distribute Go code. Introduced in Go 1.11, modules handle the versioning of dependencies and eliminate the need for $GOPATH restrictions, providing more flexibility in managing projects.

1. **What is a Go Module?**

A **module** is a collection of Go packages stored in a file tree. The root of a module contains a go.mod file that defines the module's properties, including dependencies.

2. **Creating a New Module**

To create a new module, navigate to your project directory and run:

```sh
Copy code
```

```
go mod init myproject
```

This creates a go.mod file in your project directory, which contains information about your module.

3. **Example go.mod File**

```go
Copy code
module myproject

go 1.19
```

- **module myproject**: Defines the module name.
- **go 1.19**: Specifies the Go version.

4. **Using Modules with Dependencies**
When you add a new import that is not part of the standard library, Go automatically downloads the dependency and updates go.mod.

- **Adding a Dependency:**

```go
Copy code
import "github.com/google/uuid"
```

- Running the program will automatically update go.mod and create a go.sum file to record the dependency versions.

Importing and Managing Dependencies
Managing dependencies is critical for ensuring that your project builds consistently, regardless of the environment.

1. **Adding Dependencies**

Dependencies are automatically added to go.mod when you use them in your code and run:

```sh
Copy code
go build
```

or

```sh
Copy code
go get <dependency>
```

2. **Updating Dependencies**

To update a dependency to the latest version, use the go get command:

```sh
Copy code
go get -u github.com/google/uuid
```

3. **Tidying Up Dependencies**

Use go mod tidy to clean up unused dependencies and make sure go.mod reflects only the packages that are necessary.

```sh
Copy code
go mod tidy
```

4. **Versioning in go.mod**

The go.mod file will include version numbers for dependencies to ensure consistency across builds. You can specify a specific version if required.

- **Example:**

```go
Copy code
require github.com/google/uuid v1.3.0
```

5. **Private Modules**
If you need to work with private repositories, you can set up authentication or proxy configurations in your Go environment to access them securely.
Best Practices for Packages and Modules

1. **Organize Code Logically**:

- Group related functions into packages for easier maintenance and readability.
- Avoid putting too much code in the main package.

1. **Use Exported/Unexported Conventions**:

- Export only what is necessary for other packages to use. Keep internal details unexported to enforce encapsulation.

1. **Manage Dependencies with Care**:

- Use go.mod to maintain consistent versions of dependencies across environments.
- Use go mod tidy regularly to ensure unused packages do not inflate your codebase.

1. **Avoid Circular Dependencies**:

- Go does not support circular imports. Structure packages in such a way that dependencies do not form a loop.

Chapter 10: File Handling and I/O

File handling is a fundamental part of many programs, allowing applications to read data from or write data to files. In this chapter, we will explore how to perform basic file operations, work with buffers to enhance I/O efficiency, manage JSON and XML data, and handle file permissions and errors effectively.

Reading and Writing Files in Go

The os and io/ioutil packages in Go provide easy ways to work with files. Here's how to perform the most common file operations: reading, writing, appending, and closing files.

1. **Reading Files**

The os and bufio packages provide ways to read the contents of a file.

- **Example: Reading an Entire File**

```go
Copy code
import (
    "fmt"
    "io/ioutil"
    "os"
)
```

```go
func main() {
    data, err := ioutil.ReadFile("example.txt")
    if err != nil {
        fmt.Println("Error reading file:", err)
        return
    }
    fmt.Println(string(data))
}
```

- ioutil.ReadFile() reads the entire file and returns its contents as a byte slice.
- **Reading File Line by Line Using bufio:**

```go
Copy code
import (
    "bufio"
    "fmt"
    "os"
)

func main() {
    file, err := os.Open("example.txt")
    if err != nil {
        fmt.Println("Error opening file:", err)
        return
    }
    defer file.Close()

    scanner := bufio.NewScanner(file)
    for scanner.Scan() {
        fmt.Println(scanner.Text())
    }

    if err := scanner.Err(); err != nil {
        fmt.Println("Error reading file:", err)
```

CHAPTER 10: FILE HANDLING AND I/O

}
}

- **bufio.NewScanner()** helps in reading the file line by line, making it more memory efficient for large files.

2. Writing Files

The os package provides functions to create and write to files.

- **Writing Data to a File:**

```go
import (
    "fmt"
    "os"
)

func main() {
    file, err := os.Create("example.txt")
    if err != nil {
        fmt.Println("Error creating file:", err)
        return
    }
    defer file.Close()

    _, err = file.WriteString("Hello, Go!\n")
    if err != nil {
        fmt.Println("Error writing to file:", err)
    }
}
```

- **os.Create()** creates a file or truncates it if it already exists.
- **file.WriteString()** writes a string to the file.

3. Appending to Files

To append to a file, you can use os.OpenFile() with the appropriate flag.

- **Example: Appending Data:**

```go
Copy code
func main() {
    file, err := os.OpenFile("example.txt", 
    os.O_APPEND|os.O_WRONLY, 0644)
    if err != nil {
        fmt.Println("Error opening file for appending:", err)
        return
    }
    defer file.Close()

    _, err = file.WriteString("Appending new line\n")
    if err != nil {
        fmt.Println("Error writing to file:", err)
    }
}
```

- **Flags (os.O_APPEND | os.O_WRONLY)** indicate that the file should be opened for writing and that new content should be appended.

Working with Buffers

Buffers can be used to improve efficiency when reading or writing large amounts of data. The bufio package provides buffered readers and writers to optimize I/O operations.

1. Buffered Writing

Buffered writing improves performance by reducing the number of write operations.

- **Example: Using bufio.Writer**

```go
Copy code
import (
    "bufio"
    "fmt"
    "os"
)

func main() {
    file, err := os.Create("buffered_example.txt")
    if err != nil {
        fmt.Println("Error creating file:", err)
        return
    }
    defer file.Close()

    writer := bufio.NewWriter(file)
    _, err = writer.WriteString("Buffered write example\n")
    if err != nil {
        fmt.Println("Error writing to buffer:", err)
    }

    // Flush the buffer to ensure all data is written to the file
    writer.Flush()
}
```

2. Buffered Reading

Buffered reading allows you to read larger chunks of data at once, improving performance for large files.

- **Example: Using bufio.Reader**

```go
Copy code
import (
    "bufio"
```

```go
    "fmt"
    "os"
)

func main() {
    file, err := os.Open("example.txt")
    if err != nil {
        fmt.Println("Error opening file:", err)
        return
    }
    defer file.Close()

    reader := bufio.NewReader(file)
    line, err := reader.ReadString('\n')
    if err != nil {
        fmt.Println("Error reading line:", err)
    }
    fmt.Println(line)
}
```

Working with JSON and XML Files

JSON and XML are common data formats, and Go's encoding/json and encoding/xml packages make it easy to work with them.

1. **Working with JSON**

   - **Reading and Writing JSON:**

```go
Copy code
import (
    "encoding/json"
    "fmt"
    "os"
)

type Person struct {
```

```
    Name string `json:"name"`
    Age  int    `json:"age"`
}

func main() {
    // Writing JSON to a file
    p := Person{Name: "Alice", Age: 30}
    file, _ := os.Create("person.json")
    defer file.Close()

    encoder := json.NewEncoder(file)
    encoder.Encode(p)

    // Reading JSON from a file
    file, _ = os.Open("person.json")
    defer file.Close()

    var p2 Person
    decoder := json.NewDecoder(file)
    decoder.Decode(&p2)

    fmt.Printf("Read Person: %+v\n", p2)
}
```

- **json.NewEncoder() and json.NewDecoder()** handle encoding and decoding JSON to and from files.
- Struct tags (json:"name") specify how fields should be represented in the JSON output.

2. **Working with XML**

- **Reading and Writing XML:**

```go
Copy code
import (
    "encoding/xml"
    "fmt"
    "os"
)

type Employee struct {
    XMLName xml.Name `xml:"employee"`
    Name    string   `xml:"name"`
    Age     int      `xml:"age"`
}

func main() {
    // Writing XML to a file
    e := Employee{Name: "Bob", Age: 35}
    file, _ := os.Create("employee.xml")
    defer file.Close()

    encoder := xml.NewEncoder(file)
    encoder.Encode(e)

    // Reading XML from a file
    file, _ = os.Open("employee.xml")
    defer file.Close()

    var e2 Employee
    decoder := xml.NewDecoder(file)
    decoder.Decode(&e2)

    fmt.Printf("Read Employee: %+v\n", e2)
}
```

- **xml.NewEncoder() and xml.NewDecoder()** are used for encoding and decoding XML data.
- Struct tags (xml:"name") define the XML representation of the fields.

CHAPTER 10: FILE HANDLING AND I/O

File Permissions and Error Handling
When working with files, it's crucial to handle permissions correctly to prevent runtime errors and unauthorized access.

1. **File Permissions**
File permissions are represented by a 3-digit octal number. For example, 0644 gives the owner read and write permissions, and others read-only permission.

- **Example: Creating a File with Permissions**

```go
Copy code
file, err := os.OpenFile("example.txt", os.O_CREATE|os.O_WRONLY, 0644)
if err != nil {
    fmt.Println("Error creating file:", err)
    return
}
defer file.Close()
```

2. **Handling Errors**
Error handling is crucial when working with file operations. Functions from the os package return an error if the operation fails, and these errors should always be checked to handle issues gracefully.

- **Checking for Errors:**

```go
Copy code
func main() {
    file, err := os.Open("non_existent_file.txt")
    if err != nil {
        fmt.Println("Error:", err)
```

```go
        return
    }
    defer file.Close()
}
```

3. Handling Specific Errors with os.IsNotExist

The os package provides helper functions for identifying specific types of errors, such as checking if a file does not exist.

- **Example: Handling File Not Found:**

```go
Copy code
_, err := os.Open("non_existent.txt")
if os.IsNotExist(err) {
    fmt.Println("File does not exist")
}
```

4. Deleting Files

You can use os.Remove() to delete a file.

- **Example:**

```go
Copy code
err := os.Remove("example.txt")
if err != nil {
    fmt.Println("Error deleting file:", err)
}
```

Chapter 11: Testing and Benchmarking in Go

Testing is an essential part of software development, ensuring that your code works as expected and preventing regressions. Go includes a built-in testing framework that makes it easy to write unit tests, benchmarks, and more. This chapter will cover an introduction to Go's testing framework, writing unit tests, benchmarking your code, and creating table-driven tests.

Introduction to Go's Testing Framework

Go's testing framework is provided by the testing package, which comes with the Go standard library. The go test command runs test functions defined in your Go code and provides output that helps identify errors or performance issues.

1. **The testing Package**

The testing package provides tools for writing tests and benchmarks. Test files must end with _test.go, and test functions should start with the prefix Test.

- **Basic Test File Structure**:
  - Test files end with _test.go (e.g., mathutils_test.go).
  - Test functions follow the naming convention func TestXxx(t *testing.T).
  - Import the testing package to create test cases.

- **Example Test File** (mathutils_test.go):

```go
Copy code
package mathutils

import "testing"

func TestAdd(t *testing.T) {
    result := Add(2, 3)
    if result != 5 {
        t.Errorf("Expected 5, but got %d", result)
    }
}
```

2. **Running Tests**

Use the go test command to run your tests.

- **Command**:

```sh
Copy code
go test
```

- **Output**: If the tests pass, the output will simply state ok, but if any tests fail, detailed information about the failure will be shown.

Writing Unit Tests with the testing Package

Unit tests are used to verify the correctness of individual units of code, like functions or methods. Go's testing framework is well-suited to write effective unit tests.

1. **Creating a Unit Test**

Unit tests in Go are written by defining functions that take a *testing.T as a parameter. The t object is used to report failures.

- **Example: Writing a Unit Test for an Add Function**:

```go
package mathutils

import "testing"

func TestAdd(t *testing.T) {
    result := Add(5, 5)
    expected := 10
    if result != expected {
        t.Errorf("Add(5, 5) = %d; want %d", result, expected)
    }
}
```

- **t.Errorf()**: This is used to indicate a test failure, displaying an error message with expected and actual results.

2. **Common Testing Methods**

- **t.Fail()**: Marks the test as failed but continues execution.
- **t.FailNow()**: Marks the test as failed and stops execution.
- **t.Log() and t.Logf()**: Used for logging additional information during tests.

3. **Organizing Test Files**

To keep tests organized, put them in the same package and directory as the code they are testing, but with the filename ending in _test.go.

Benchmarking Your Code

Benchmarking allows you to measure the performance of your code. Go provides the B type in the testing package to help create benchmarks.

1. **Writing a Benchmark**

Benchmark functions must start with the prefix Benchmark and take a *testing.B as a parameter. The b object is used to control and measure how long the benchmark runs.

- **Example: Benchmarking an Add Function:**

```go
Copy code
package mathutils

import "testing"

func BenchmarkAdd(b *testing.B) {
    for i := 0; i < b.N; i++ {
        Add(5, 5)
    }
}
```

- **b.N**: The number of iterations the function should run. The Go testing framework determines this automatically to produce accurate measurements.

2. **Running Benchmarks**

To run benchmarks, use the -bench flag followed by the name of the function or . to run all benchmarks.

- **Command**:

```sh
Copy code
go test -bench=.
```

- **Output**: Benchmark results include the number of iterations and the average time taken per operation.

3. **Example Output**:

```bash
Copy code
BenchmarkAdd-8      2000000000      0.25 ns/op
```

This indicates the benchmark ran for 2 billion iterations with an average of 0.25 nanoseconds per iteration.

Writing Table-Driven Tests

Table-driven tests are a common pattern in Go for writing multiple test cases efficiently. This pattern is particularly useful when testing a function with multiple inputs and expected outputs.

1. **Creating Table-Driven Tests**

Table-driven tests use a slice of structs to store test cases, making it easy to add or remove cases.

- **Example: Table-Driven Test for Add Function**:

```go
Copy code
package mathutils

import "testing"
```

```go
func TestAdd(t *testing.T) {
    tests := []struct {
        name     string
        a, b     int
        expected int
    }{
        {"positive numbers", 1, 2, 3},
        {"zero and positive", 0, 5, 5},
        {"negative numbers", -1, -1, -2},
        {"positive and negative", 4, -2, 2},
    }

    for _, tt := range tests {
        t.Run(tt.name, func(t *testing.T) {
            result := Add(tt.a, tt.b)
            if result != tt.expected {
                t.Errorf("Add(%d, %d) = %d; want %d", tt.a, tt.b,
                    result, tt.expected)
            }
        })
    }
}
```

- **t.Run()**: This function allows each test case to run as a subtest, making it easier to identify which test failed.
- **tests slice**: A slice of structs defines each test case, including the inputs and expected output.

2. Advantages of Table-Driven Tests

- **Easier to Manage**: New test cases can be added easily without duplicating test code.
- **Readable**: Test cases are well-organized and easy to understand.

3. Example: Testing Edge Cases:

Using table-driven tests helps in covering a wide range of scenarios, including edge cases like negative numbers, zeros, or large inputs, with minimal repetition.

Best Practices for Testing in Go

1. **Write Tests Early**:

- Writing tests alongside your code helps catch bugs early and makes it easier to refactor confidently.

1. **Aim for High Coverage**:

- Use go test -cover to check the coverage of your tests, and ensure you're testing critical parts of your code.

1. **Use Table-Driven Tests for Flexibility**:

- Whenever possible, use table-driven tests to manage multiple test scenarios efficiently.

1. **Benchmark Critical Code Paths**:

- Use benchmarks to identify performance bottlenecks, especially for code that is run frequently or that handles large amounts of data.

1. **Avoid Overuse of t.Fatal**:

- t.Fatal() immediately stops the test, so use it only for conditions where continuing makes no sense.

Chapter 12: Go with Web Development

Go is well-known for its simplicity and performance in web development. With its built-in packages like net/http and support for concurrent handling, Go makes building web applications straightforward and efficient. In this chapter, we will explore building web applications, handling HTTP requests, working with templates, implementing routing and middleware, and creating JSON APIs.

Building Web Applications with Go

Web development in Go often involves building a server to handle HTTP requests and generating responses. The core of Go's web capabilities is the net/http package, which provides everything you need to build a basic web server.

1. **Setting Up a Web Server**

Go's net/http package is at the heart of web development in Go. To create a simple web server, you need to set up routes and define handlers to manage incoming requests.

- **Example: A Basic Web Server**:

```go
Copy code
```

CHAPTER 12: GO WITH WEB DEVELOPMENT

```go
package main

import (
    "fmt"
    "net/http"
)

func handler(w http.ResponseWriter, r *http.Request) {
    fmt.Fprintf(w, "Hello, World!")
}

func main() {
    http.HandleFunc("/", handler)   // Register the handler
    function for the root path
    fmt.Println("Starting server at port 8080...")
    http.ListenAndServe(":8080", nil)
}
```

- **http.HandleFunc()**: Associates a path with a handler function.
- **http.ListenAndServe()**: Starts an HTTP server on the specified port.

2. **Request and Response**

In Go, handlers take an http.ResponseWriter and an http.Request as arguments:

- **http.ResponseWriter**: Used to send a response back to the client.
- **http.Request**: Provides information about the incoming request.

Serving HTTP Requests with net/http

The net/http package makes it easy to create web servers and serve content.

1. **Handling Different Routes**

To serve different pages, define multiple handlers and associate them with different paths.

- **Example: Handling Multiple Routes**:

```go
Copy code
func helloHandler(w http.ResponseWriter, r *http.Request) {
    fmt.Fprintf(w, "Hello from /hello!")
}

func aboutHandler(w http.ResponseWriter, r *http.Request) {
    fmt.Fprintf(w, "About Us Page")
}

func main() {
    http.HandleFunc("/hello", helloHandler)
    http.HandleFunc("/about", aboutHandler)
    fmt.Println("Server is running on port 8080...")
    http.ListenAndServe(":8080", nil)
}
```

- In this example, requests to /hello and /about are handled by different handler functions.

2. Handling Query Parameters

You can extract query parameters from the http.Request object.

- **Example**:

```go
Copy code
func greetHandler(w http.ResponseWriter, r *http.Request) {
    name := r.URL.Query().Get("name")
    if name == "" {
        name = "Guest"
    }
    fmt.Fprintf(w, "Hello, %s!", name)
}
```

```go
func main() {
    http.HandleFunc("/greet", greetHandler)
    http.ListenAndServe(":8080", nil)
}
```

- Accessing /greet?name=Alice will display Hello, Alice!.

Understanding Templates in Go

Go's html/template package helps generate dynamic HTML pages by combining static HTML with data.

1. Using HTML Templates

Templates make it easy to separate the HTML presentation from Go logic. Templates in Go use placeholders to insert dynamic data.

- **Creating a Simple Template**:

```go
Copy code
import (
    "html/template"
    "net/http"
)

func main() {
    tmpl := template.Must(template.ParseFiles("index.html"))

    http.HandleFunc("/", func(w http.ResponseWriter, r *http.Request) {
        data := struct {
            Title string
            Name  string
        }{
```

```
            Title: "Welcome Page",
            Name:  "Guest",
        }
        tmpl.Execute(w, data)
    })

    http.ListenAndServe(":8080", nil)
}
```

- **template.Must()**: Ensures the template is parsed correctly and panics if it fails.
- **tmpl.Execute()**: Renders the template with the provided data.

2. **Template Syntax**

Go templates use {{}} to denote template actions.

- **Basic Template Example (index.html):**

```html
Copy code
<!DOCTYPE html>
<html>
<head>
    <title>{{ .Title }}</title>
</head>
<body>
    <h1>Hello, {{ .Name }}!</h1>
</body>
</html>
```

- The {{ .Title }} and {{ .Name }} placeholders are replaced with values from the data struct.

Routing and Middleware
As web applications grow, it becomes necessary to manage routes efficiently and apply middleware to handle cross-cutting concerns like logging, authentication, and request validation.

1. **Routing with a Framework**

Although Go's net/http provides basic routing, frameworks like **Gorilla Mux** offer more powerful routing capabilities.

- **Using Gorilla Mux**:

```go
Copy code
import (
    "fmt"
    "net/http"
    "github.com/gorilla/mux"
)

func main() {
    r := mux.NewRouter()
    r.HandleFunc("/products/{id}", func(w http.ResponseWriter, r *http.Request) {
        vars := mux.Vars(r)
        id := vars["id"]
        fmt.Fprintf(w, "Product ID: %s", id)
    })
    http.ListenAndServe(":8080", r)
}
```

- **Path Parameters**: Mux allows defining paths with parameters (/products/{id}), which are easily retrieved using mux.Vars().

2. **Middleware**

Middleware functions are used to perform tasks before or after the main request handler runs.

- **Example Middleware for Logging**:

```go
func loggingMiddleware(next http.Handler) http.Handler {
    return http.HandlerFunc(func(w http.ResponseWriter, r
    *http.Request) {
        fmt.Printf("Request: %s %s\n", r.Method, r.URL.Path)
        next.ServeHTTP(w, r)
    })
}

func main() {
    r := mux.NewRouter()
    r.Use(loggingMiddleware)
    r.HandleFunc("/", func(w http.ResponseWriter, r *http.Request)
    {
        fmt.Fprintln(w, "Home Page")
    })
    http.ListenAndServe(":8080", r)
}
```

- In this example, every incoming request passes through the loggingMiddleware before reaching the main handler.

JSON APIs in Go

Building APIs that work with JSON is one of the most common tasks in web development. Go provides the encoding/json package to work easily with JSON data.

1. **Creating a JSON API Endpoint**

The encoding/json package makes it straightforward to encode Go structs to JSON and decode JSON to Go structs.

- **Example: Returning JSON Response**:

```go
Copy code
import (
    "encoding/json"
    "net/http"
)

type Product struct {
    ID    string  `json:"id"`
    Name  string  `json:"name"`
    Price float64 `json:"price"`
}

func productHandler(w http.ResponseWriter, r *http.Request) {
    product := Product{ID: "123", Name: "Laptop", Price: 799.99}
    w.Header().Set("Content-Type", "application/json")
    json.NewEncoder(w).Encode(product)
}

func main() {
    http.HandleFunc("/product", productHandler)
    http.ListenAndServe(":8080", nil)
}
```

- **json.NewEncoder(w).Encode(product)**: Encodes a Go struct to JSON and writes it to http.ResponseWriter.
- **Setting Content-Type**: It is important to set the correct Content-Type header when returning JSON ("application/json").

2. **Handling JSON Requests**

To handle incoming JSON requests, use json.NewDecoder() to parse the request body into a Go struct.

- **Example: Handling JSON Input**:

```go
Copy code
func createProductHandler(w http.ResponseWriter, r *http.Request) {
    var product Product
    err := json.NewDecoder(r.Body).Decode(&product)
    if err != nil {
        http.Error(w, "Invalid input", http.StatusBadRequest)
        return
    }
    fmt.Fprintf(w, "Product created: %+v\n", product)
}

func main() {
    http.HandleFunc("/create", createProductHandler)
    http.ListenAndServe(":8080", nil)
}
```

- **json.NewDecoder(r.Body).Decode(&product)**: Decodes the JSON body into the product struct.
- **Error Handling**: Return an error response if the input is invalid.

3. Handling HTTP Methods

You can easily create RESTful endpoints by checking the HTTP method in your handler.

- **Example: Method Checking**:

```go
Copy code
func main() {
    http.HandleFunc("/product", func(w http.ResponseWriter, r *http.Request) {
        switch r.Method {
```

```go
        case http.MethodGet:
            // Handle GET
            fmt.Fprintln(w, "Getting product")
        case http.MethodPost:
            // Handle POST
            fmt.Fprintln(w, "Creating product")
        default:
            http.Error(w, "Method Not Allowed",
            http.StatusMethodNotAllowed)
        }
    })
    http.ListenAndServe(":8080", nil)
}
```

Chapter 13: Working with Databases

Databases are fundamental to building dynamic, data-driven applications. In Go, working with databases is straightforward, thanks to the database/sql package and other tools that provide abstraction layers for interacting with databases. This chapter will cover how to connect Go with databases, use SQL, work with ORM tools such as GORM and sqlx, and perform basic CRUD (Create, Read, Update, Delete) operations.

Connecting Go with Databases

To connect to a database in Go, you typically use the database/sql package, which provides a general-purpose interface for SQL databases. You also need a **driver** specific to the database you are using (e.g., PostgreSQL, MySQL).

1. **Importing Required Packages**
- **database/sql**: The core package to work with SQL databases.
- **Driver**: A driver is required to connect to the specific database. Popular drivers include:
- **PostgreSQL**: github.com/lib/pq
- **MySQL**: github.com/go-sql-driver/mysql

2. **Connecting to a Database**

The connection to a database is established using the sql.Open() function, which takes the driver name and the data source name (DSN).

CHAPTER 13: WORKING WITH DATABASES

- **Example: Connecting to a PostgreSQL Database:**

```go
import (
    "database/sql"
    "fmt"
    _ "github.com/lib/pq" // PostgreSQL driver
)

func main() {
    connStr := "user=username dbname=mydb sslmode=disable password=mypassword"
    db, err := sql.Open("postgres", connStr)
    if err != nil {
        fmt.Println("Error connecting to the database:", err)
        return
    }
    defer db.Close()

    err = db.Ping()
    if err != nil {
        fmt.Println("Error pinging the database:", err)
        return
    }

    fmt.Println("Successfully connected to the database!")
}
```

- **sql.Open()**: Opens a connection to the database. It doesn't create a connection immediately but validates the parameters.
- **db.Ping()**: Verifies that the connection to the database is established correctly.

3. Database Connection Pooling

sql.Open() provides connection pooling by default, which means multiple clients can reuse the same connection, increasing efficiency. It is recommended to configure the max open connections and idle connections for optimal performance.

- **Example:**

```go
Copy code
db.SetMaxOpenConns(25)
db.SetMaxIdleConns(25)
db.SetConnMaxLifetime(5 * time.Minute)
```

Using SQL with Go

Once connected, you can use SQL statements to interact with the database using methods such as Query(), QueryRow(), and Exec().

1. **Executing Queries**

- **Exec()**: Executes SQL statements that do not return rows (e.g., INSERT, UPDATE, DELETE).
- **Query()**: Executes SQL queries that return multiple rows (e.g., SELECT).
- **QueryRow()**: Executes a SQL query that is expected to return a single row.
- **Example: Creating a Table:**

```go
Copy code
query := `
    CREATE TABLE IF NOT EXISTS users (
        id SERIAL PRIMARY KEY,
        name TEXT,
        age INT
    );`
```

CHAPTER 13: WORKING WITH DATABASES

```go
_, err := db.Exec(query)
if err != nil {
    fmt.Println("Error creating table:", err)
}
```

2. Querying Data

Query() and QueryRow() are used to fetch data from the database. Query() returns multiple rows, while QueryRow() returns only a single row.

- **Example: Selecting Multiple Rows**:

```go
Copy code
rows, err := db.Query("SELECT id, name, age FROM users")
if err != nil {
    fmt.Println("Error querying users:", err)
    return
}
defer rows.Close()

for rows.Next() {
    var id int
    var name string
    var age int
    if err := rows.Scan(&id, &name, &age); err != nil {
        fmt.Println("Error scanning row:", err)
        return
    }
    fmt.Printf("ID: %d, Name: %s, Age: %d\n", id, name, age)
}
```

3. Inserting Data

- **Example: Inserting Data**:

115

```go
Copy code
_, err := db.Exec("INSERT INTO users (name, age) VALUES ($1, $2)",
"Alice", 30)
if err != nil {
    fmt.Println("Error inserting data:", err)
}
```

ORM Tools in Go: GORM and sqlx

Object Relational Mappers (ORMs) simplify the interaction with databases by allowing you to work with Go structs instead of SQL queries. Two popular ORM tools in Go are **GORM** and **sqlx**.

1. GORM

GORM is a powerful and popular ORM library for Go that provides a wide range of features for working with databases.

- **Installation**:

```sh
Copy code
go get -u gorm.io/gorm
go get -u gorm.io/driver/postgres
```

- **Basic Usage**:

```go
Copy code
import (
    "gorm.io/driver/postgres"
    "gorm.io/gorm"
    "fmt"
)
```

```go
type User struct {
    ID   uint   `gorm:"primaryKey"`
    Name string
    Age  int
}

func main() {
    dsn := "user=username password=mypassword dbname=mydb
    port=5432 sslmode=disable"
    db, err := gorm.Open(postgres.Open(dsn), &gorm.Config{})
    if err != nil {
        fmt.Println("Failed to connect to database:", err)
        return
    }

    // Auto migrate to create/update the schema
    db.AutoMigrate(&User{})

    // Insert data
    db.Create(&User{Name: "Bob", Age: 28})

    // Read data
    var user User
    db.First(&user, 1) // find user with ID 1
    fmt.Printf("User found: %+v\n", user)
}
```

2. sqlx

sqlx is an extension to Go's database/sql that provides additional features like struct scanning.

- **Installation**:

```sh
Copy code
```

go get github.com/jmoiron/sqlx

- **Basic Usage**:

go
Copy code
```
import (
    "fmt"
    "github.com/jmoiron/sqlx"
    _ "github.com/lib/pq"
)

type User struct {
    ID   int    `db:"id"`
    Name string `db:"name"`
    Age  int    `db:"age"`
}

func main() {
    db, err := sqlx.Connect("postgres", "user=username dbname=mydb sslmode=disable password=mypassword")
    if err != nil {
        fmt.Println("Error connecting to the database:", err)
        return
    }

    var users []User
    err = db.Select(&users, "SELECT id, name, age FROM users")
    if err != nil {
        fmt.Println("Error selecting users:", err)
        return
    }

    for _, user := range users {
        fmt.Printf("User: %+v\n", user)
    }
}
```

- **Struct Tags** (db:"name"): Used to map columns in the database to struct fields.

CRUD Operations in Go

CRUD (Create, Read, Update, Delete) operations are the foundation for interacting with databases. Here's how to perform each of these operations using Go's database/sql.

1. **Create**

Insert a new record into the database.

- **Example**:

```go
Copy code
_, err := db.Exec("INSERT INTO users (name, age) VALUES ($1, $2)", "Charlie", 22)
if err != nil {
    fmt.Println("Error inserting user:", err)
}
```

2. **Read**

Select data from the database using QueryRow() or Query().

- **Example**:

```go
Copy code
var name string
var age int
err := db.QueryRow("SELECT name, age FROM users WHERE id = $1", 1).Scan(&name, &age)
if err != nil {
```

```go
    fmt.Println("Error querying user:", err)
}
fmt.Printf("User: %s, Age: %d\n", name, age)
```

3. **Update**

Update existing records in the database.

- **Example**:

```go
Copy code
_, err := db.Exec("UPDATE users SET age = $1 WHERE name = $2", 29, "Charlie")
if err != nil {
    fmt.Println("Error updating user:", err)
}
```

4. **Delete**

Delete a record from the database.

- **Example**:

```go
Copy code
_, err := db.Exec("DELETE FROM users WHERE name = $1", "Charlie")
if err != nil {
    fmt.Println("Error deleting user:", err)
}
```

Best Practices for Working with Databases in Go

1. **Use Prepared Statements**: To prevent SQL injection attacks, use prepared statements.

CHAPTER 13: WORKING WITH DATABASES

```go
stmt, err := db.Prepare("INSERT INTO users(name, age) VALUES($1, $2)")
if err != nil {
    log.Fatal(err)
}
defer stmt.Close()
_, err = stmt.Exec("Alice", 30)
```

1. **Connection Management**: Use SetMaxOpenConns, SetMaxIdleConns, and SetConnMaxLifetime to optimize your database connection pool.
2. **Use Transactions for Multiple Operations**: For complex operations involving multiple SQL commands, use transactions.

```go
tx, err := db.Begin()
if err != nil {
    log.Fatal(err)
}

_, err = tx.Exec("UPDATE accounts SET balance = balance - $1 WHERE id = $2", 100, 1)
if err != nil {
    tx.Rollback()  // Rollback on error
    log.Fatal(err)
}

err = tx.Commit()
if err != nil {
    log.Fatal(err)
}
```

121

Chapter 14: Error Logging and Debugging

Error logging and debugging are critical skills for any software developer, helping you identify and fix problems quickly and ensure that your Go applications run efficiently. In this chapter, we will explore how to log errors and debug Go applications using the log package and third-party libraries, as well as various debugging techniques and tools available for Go, including profiling and optimization for performance.

Logging Errors and Debugging Go Applications

Proper error logging helps in maintaining the visibility of your application's state during runtime, making debugging more manageable. Go's built-in log package is simple yet powerful for logging, and there are more advanced third-party libraries for sophisticated logging requirements.

1. Why Log Errors?

Logging errors is crucial for understanding what went wrong in your application and under what circumstances:

- **Error Tracking**: Logs can help you identify and track errors over time.
- **Debugging**: Logs provide insights that are invaluable during debugging.
- **Operational Monitoring**: Logs help monitor application performance and catch issues before they escalate.

2. Using the log Package

The log package provides a basic interface for logging information.

CHAPTER 14: ERROR LOGGING AND DEBUGGING

- **Basic Logging**:

```go
Copy code
import (
    "log"
)

func main() {
    log.Println("This is a log message")
    log.Fatal("This is a fatal log message")  // Logs message and
    calls os.Exit(1)
}
```

- **log.Println()**: Logs a message with a timestamp.
- **log.Fatal()**: Logs a message and exits the program immediately.
- **log.Panic()**: Logs the message and then panics.

3. **Customizing the Log Output**

You can customize the log output to include additional information such as timestamps, file names, and line numbers.

- **Example: Setting Log Flags**:

```go
Copy code
import (
    "log"
)

func main() {
    log.SetFlags(log.Ldate | log.Ltime | log.Lshortfile)
    log.Println("Customized log message")
```

123

}

- **log.Ldate**: Adds the date to log entries.
- **log.Ltime**: Adds the time to log entries.
- **log.Lshortfile**: Adds the file name and line number to log entries.

4. **Using Log Files**

Instead of logging to standard output, you can log messages to a file.

- **Example: Logging to a File:**

```go
Copy code
import (
    "log"
    "os"
)

func main() {
    file, err := os.OpenFile("app.log",
    os.O_APPEND|os.O_CREATE|os.O_WRONLY, 0666)
    if err != nil {
        log.Fatal(err)
    }
    defer file.Close()

    log.SetOutput(file)
    log.Println("Logging to a file")
}
```

The log Package and Third-Party Logging Libraries

While the standard log package is adequate for simple applications, third-party libraries provide more advanced features, such as structured logging, log levels, and support for distributed environments.

1. **Third-Party Logging Libraries**

CHAPTER 14: ERROR LOGGING AND DEBUGGING

- **Logrus**: A popular structured logging library for Go that provides leveled logging.
- **Zap**: A high-performance, structured logging library by Uber, designed for efficiency.
- **Zerolog**: A fast, JSON-based logging library for structured logging.

2. Using Logrus

Logrus provides structured logging with levels like Info, Warn, Error, etc.

- **Installation**:

```sh
sh
Copy code
go get github.com/sirupsen/logrus
```

- **Basic Example**:

```go
go
Copy code
import (
    "github.com/sirupsen/logrus"
)

func main() {
    logrus.SetFormatter(&logrus.JSONFormatter{})
    logrus.SetLevel(logrus.InfoLevel)

    logrus.Info("This is an info message")
    logrus.Warn("This is a warning")
    logrus.WithFields(logrus.Fields{
        "user": "Alice",
        "age":  30,
```

```
            }).Info("User details")
        }
```

- **WithFields()**: Adds structured context to log messages.

3. Using Zap

Zap provides fast and structured logging, ideal for production environments.

- **Installation**:

```sh
Copy code
go get go.uber.org/zap
```

- **Basic Example**:

```go
Copy code
import (
    "go.uber.org/zap"
)

func main() {
    logger, _ := zap.NewProduction()
    defer logger.Sync()

    logger.Info("Logging with zap", zap.String("module", "main"))
    logger.Error("This is an error message", zap.Int("status",
    500))
}
```

CHAPTER 14: ERROR LOGGING AND DEBUGGING

Debugging Techniques and Tools

Debugging is crucial for understanding the runtime behavior of your application and fixing any issues effectively.

1. **Debugging with fmt Statements**

Adding fmt.Println() statements is the simplest way to understand code flow and values, but it is not ideal for complex issues or production environments.

2. **Using Go's Built-in Debugger: delve**

Delve is the official debugger for Go. It allows setting breakpoints, stepping through code, and inspecting variables.

- **Installing Delve**:

```sh
Copy code
go install github.com/go-delve/delve/cmd/dlv@latest
```

- **Running Delve**: To debug a Go program:

```sh
Copy code
dlv debug main.go
```

- **Breakpoints**: Set breakpoints to pause execution at specific lines.
- **Step Through Code**: Use next and step commands to move through the program.
- **Inspect Variables**: Use the print command to inspect variable values.

3. **Debugging with VSCode**

If you're using Visual Studio Code, you can use the **Go extension** for debugging. This extension integrates with Delve, allowing you to set breakpoints, inspect variables, and control program execution.

Profiling and Optimization

Profiling helps understand where a program is spending most of its time or memory, which is critical for optimizing performance.

1. **Profiling with pprof**

The net/http/pprof package provides profiling tools for CPU usage, memory usage, and goroutine analysis.

- **Importing pprof:**

```go
Copy code
import _ "net/http/pprof"
```

- **Adding Profiling to an Application:**

```go
Copy code
import (
    "net/http"
    _ "net/http/pprof"
)

func main() {
    go func() {
        log.Println(http.ListenAndServe("localhost:6060", nil))
    }()
    // Rest of your application code
}
```

- This starts an HTTP server on port 6060 for profiling.

- **Accessing Profiles**: You can access profiling data by visiting http://localhost:6060/debug/pprof.

2. CPU Profiling Example

CPU profiling provides insights into which functions are consuming the most CPU time.

- **Example: Generating CPU Profile**:

```go
Copy code
import (
    "os"
    "runtime/pprof"
)

func main() {
    f, err := os.Create("cpu.prof")
    if err != nil {
        log.Fatal(err)
    }
    defer f.Close()

    pprof.StartCPUProfile(f)
    defer pprof.StopCPUProfile()

    // Application code that you want to profile
}
```

- **pprof.StartCPUProfile()**: Starts capturing CPU profile data.
- **pprof.StopCPUProfile()**: Stops profiling and writes data to the file.

3. Memory Profiling Example

Memory profiling helps identify memory leaks and understand the memory allocation of your application.

- **Example: Generating Memory Profile:**

```go
Copy code
import (
    "os"
    "runtime"
    "runtime/pprof"
)

func main() {
    // Your application code

    f, err := os.Create("mem.prof")
    if err != nil {
        log.Fatal(err)
    }
    defer f.Close()

    runtime.GC() // Trigger garbage collection to get an accurate picture of memory usage
    pprof.WriteHeapProfile(f)
}
```

4. **Analyzing Profiles with go tool pprof**

To analyze the profile files, use go tool pprof.

- **Command:**

```sh
Copy code
go tool pprof cpu.prof
```

- This command opens an interactive terminal where you can use commands like top, list, and web to analyze the profiling data.

Best Practices for Logging and Debugging

1. **Use Log Levels**: Use different log levels (Info, Warn, Error, Debug) to categorize messages and adjust verbosity.
2. **Avoid Logging Sensitive Data**: Do not log passwords, secrets, or any sensitive information.
3. **Use Context in Logs**: Include contextual information like request IDs or user IDs to make debugging easier.
4. **Automate Log Monitoring**: Use log aggregation and monitoring tools (like ELK Stack, Graylog, or Splunk) to track logs and identify issues proactively.
5. **Keep Logs Manageable**: Use a log rotation system to prevent your logs from consuming too much disk space.

Chapter 15: Deployment and Best Practices

In this chapter, we will discuss how to package and deploy Go applications, cross-compile Go programs for different platforms, and follow best practices for writing clean and maintainable Go code. This includes managing dependencies, versioning, and writing idiomatic Go that is easy to read and maintain.

Packaging and Deploying Go Applications

Packaging and deployment are crucial steps to ensure that your Go application reaches users effectively. Go provides tools that simplify building standalone executables, making deployment straightforward.

1. Building Go Applications

The go build command compiles Go source code into an executable. This executable is a statically linked binary, which makes Go applications easy to deploy without needing external dependencies.

- **Example: Building an Application**:

sh
Copy code

```
go build -o myapp main.go
```

- **-o flag**: Specifies the name of the output file.
- This command will produce a binary named myapp.

2. Deploying Go Applications

Since Go applications are compiled into standalone binaries, deployment often involves copying the binary and relevant configuration files to a server.

- **Deployment Steps**:

1. **Build the Application**: Use go build to create the binary.
2. **Transfer the Binary**: Transfer the binary to the target server using tools like **scp** or **rsync**.
3. **Set Up Environment**: Configure environment variables using a .env file or system-level settings.
4. **Run the Application**: Start the application with a process manager like **systemd**, **supervisor**, or a container runtime if deploying in a container.

3. Containerizing Go Applications

Docker is commonly used to containerize applications. A Dockerfile defines the image and its environment.

- **Example Dockerfile**:

```
dockerfile
Copy code
# Use the official Golang image as a base
FROM golang:1.19 AS build

# Set the working directory
```

```
WORKDIR /app

# Copy the Go modules and download dependencies
COPY go.mod go.sum ./
RUN go mod download

# Copy the rest of the code and build
COPY . .
RUN go build -o myapp

# Use a minimal base image
FROM alpine:latest
WORKDIR /root/
COPY --from=build /app/myapp .

# Run the application
CMD ["./myapp"]
```

- **Build and Run Docker Image**:

```sh
Copy code
docker build -t myapp .
docker run -p 8080:8080 myapp
```

Cross-Compiling Go Programs for Different Platforms

Go's toolchain includes built-in support for cross-compiling applications to different platforms and architectures. This means you can build binaries for Linux, macOS, and Windows from a single development machine.

1. **Setting Environment Variables**

To cross-compile, set the GOOS and GOARCH environment variables.

- **Example: Cross-Compile for Windows**:

```sh
Copy code
GOOS=windows GOARCH=amd64 go build -o myapp.exe main.go
```

- **GOOS**: Operating system (windows, linux, darwin, etc.).
- **GOARCH**: Architecture (amd64, 386, arm, etc.).

2. **Common Targets**

- **Linux 64-bit**: GOOS=linux GOARCH=amd64
- **Windows 64-bit**: GOOS=windows GOARCH=amd64
- **macOS**: GOOS=darwin GOARCH=amd64

3. **Cross-Compilation Example**

- **Example**: Cross-compiling an application for multiple platforms.

```sh
Copy code
GOOS=linux GOARCH=amd64 go build -o myapp-linux main.go
GOOS=windows GOARCH=386 go build -o myapp-windows.exe main.go
GOOS=darwin GOARCH=arm64 go build -o myapp-mac main.go
```

Best Practices for Go Code
Writing clean and idiomatic Go code improves maintainability and performance. Here are some best practices to follow when developing Go applications.

1. **Managing Dependencies and Versioning**

Go Modules is the recommended way to manage dependencies. It helps maintain consistent versions across environments and simplifies dependency management.

- **Create a Module**:

```sh
Copy code
go mod init mymodule
```

- **Add Dependencies**: When you import a package, Go automatically downloads it and adds it to the go.mod file.
- **Pinning Versions**:
- You can specify a version in go.mod to ensure consistent behavior.
- **Example**:

```go
Copy code
require github.com/sirupsen/logrus v1.8.0
```

2. Writing Clean and Idiomatic Go Code

Idiomatic Go is about following conventions established by the Go community. Some important aspects of idiomatic Go include:

- **Naming Conventions**: Use camel case for variable names (userID), keep names short but descriptive, and use uppercase for exported variables or functions.
- **Error Handling**:
- Always check for errors and handle them appropriately.
- Use fmt.Errorf to add context to an error.

```go
Copy code
if err != nil {
    return fmt.Errorf("failed to open file: %w", err)
}
```

- **Avoid Overuse of Pointers**: Use pointers only when necessary. Pointers are useful for modifying data within functions or avoiding copying large structs.
- **Use defer for Cleanup**: defer is an effective way to ensure resources like files or connections are closed properly.

```go
Copy code
file, err := os.Open("example.txt")
if err != nil {
    log.Fatal(err)
}
defer file.Close()
```

- **Prefer Short Variable Names for Short Scopes**: For example, use i, n, or err for variables that are scoped to just a few lines of code.

3. **Effective Use of Go Tools**

- **Formatting with gofmt**: Format your code using gofmt. It enforces a uniform code style.

```sh
Copy code
gofmt -w main.go
```

- **Linting with golint**: Use **golint** to catch stylistic errors and ensure your code follows best practices.
- **Static Analysis with go vet**: go vet analyzes your code to find bugs and suspicious constructs.

```sh
Copy code
go vet ./...
```

Managing Dependencies and Versioning

Managing dependencies properly is crucial to ensure your application is stable and maintainable. Go Modules (go.mod and go.sum) help with dependency tracking and versioning.

1. **Using Go Modules**

- **go.mod**: Keeps track of your dependencies.
- **go.sum**: Ensures that dependencies are exactly reproducible across different environments.
- **Adding Dependencies**:

```sh
Copy code
go get github.com/sirupsen/logrus
```

- This command adds the dependency to your project and updates go.mod and go.sum.

2. Updating Dependencies
To update a module to the latest version:

```sh
Copy code
go get -u github.com/sirupsen/logrus
```

3. Pruning Unused Dependencies
Use go mod tidy to remove unnecessary dependencies and keep go.mod clean.

```sh
Copy code
go mod tidy
```

Writing Clean and Idiomatic Go Code

1. Structuring Your Project

- **Flat Structure** for small projects.
- **Domain-Based Structure** for larger projects with different logical components.
- **Example Structure** for a REST API project:

```bash
Copy code
/myapp
    /cmd        # Entrypoints to the application
    /pkg        # Reusable packages
    /internal   # Internal code that should not be imported by external projects
```

```
/api        # API definitions, route handlers
/models     # Data models and database schema definitions
/utils      # Utility functions
main.go     # Main entry point
```

2. Conventions and Readability

- **Error Messages**: Start with a lowercase letter and avoid ending with punctuation. For example, "failed to connect to database".
- **Documentation Comments**: Provide documentation comments for packages, types, and functions that will be exported. These comments should start with the name of the item being described.
- **Small Functions**: Keep functions small and focused. This makes them easier to understand and test.

3. Concurrency Best Practices

Go's concurrency is a powerful tool, but misuse can lead to subtle bugs and deadlocks.

- **Avoid Global State**: Global state is not safe for concurrent access. Use synchronization primitives like sync.Mutex or channels.
- **Channel Guidelines**: Always close channels when done using them, and do not close a channel from multiple places.
- **Avoid Goroutine Leaks**: Ensure that goroutines are properly terminated. Use channels or context to communicate stopping signals to goroutines.

4. Effective Use of Context

The **context** package is useful for managing deadlines, cancellations, and other request-scoped values.

- **Example Usage**:

CHAPTER 15: DEPLOYMENT AND BEST PRACTICES

```go
Copy code
import (
    "context"
    "fmt"
    "time"
)

func main() {
    ctx, cancel := context.WithTimeout(context.Background(),
    2*time.Second)
    defer cancel()

    result := make(chan string)

    go func() {
        time.Sleep(1 * time.Second)
        result <- "Completed"
    }()

    select {
    case res := <-result:
        fmt.Println(res)
    case <-ctx.Done():
        fmt.Println("Timeout:", ctx.Err())
    }
}
```

- This example demonstrates using context to set a timeout, preventing a goroutine from running indefinitely.

Chapter 16: Go in the Cloud

Cloud-native development is becoming a cornerstone of software engineering, and Go, with its simplicity and performance, is a great fit for building cloud-native applications. This chapter will explore how to use Go in the cloud, covering cloud-native development concepts, deploying Go applications on popular cloud platforms (AWS, GCP, Azure), Dockerizing applications, and an introduction to Kubernetes for managing Go applications.

Go and Cloud-Native Development

Cloud-native development emphasizes scalability, resilience, and ease of deployment using cloud environments. Go's lightweight concurrency and efficient binary generation make it well-suited for cloud-native solutions.

1. **Why Go is Great for Cloud-Native Development**
   - **Performance**: Go binaries are compiled and optimized, leading to high-performance applications with lower resource consumption.
   - **Concurrency**: Goroutines and channels make Go a perfect language for handling many requests concurrently, typical for cloud services.
   - **Ease of Deployment**: Go applications compile into a single binary with minimal dependencies, simplifying deployment in cloud environments.

2. **Microservices and Go**
   Go is often used for **microservices architecture**, where each service can

be independently deployed, managed, and scaled. Its standard library is extensive, meaning you can create REST APIs, handle HTTP requests, and work with JSON with minimal external dependencies.

3. **Building Cloud-Native Go Applications**

- **Twelve-Factor App**: Build Go applications with the **twelve-factor principles** for cloud readiness:
- **Config**: Use environment variables to configure cloud environments.
- **Processes**: Stateless processes, which are ideal for scaling.
- **Logs**: Write logs to stdout/stderr, allowing the cloud environment to collect and manage them.

Deploying Go Applications on AWS, GCP, and Azure

Deploying Go applications to cloud platforms like AWS, Google Cloud Platform (GCP), and Azure requires an understanding of the services available, such as compute instances, managed container services, and serverless options.

1. **Deploying on AWS**

Amazon Web Services (AWS) provides various deployment options, including **EC2**, **Elastic Beanstalk**, and **Lambda**.

- **Deploying on EC2**:

1. **Launch an EC2 Instance**: Use the AWS Console to create an EC2 instance with your preferred Linux distribution.
2. **Transfer the Go Binary**: Use scp to transfer the compiled Go binary.
3. **Run the Application**:

```sh
Copy code
./myapp
```

1. **Configure Security Groups**: Allow inbound traffic to the application's port (e.g., port 8080).

- **Using Elastic Beanstalk**:
- Elastic Beanstalk simplifies deployment and scaling. Package your Go application, including a Procfile to define the startup command.
- **Example Procfile**:

```bash
Copy code
web: ./myapp
```

- Deploy the zip file using the AWS Elastic Beanstalk CLI or the AWS Console.
- **AWS Lambda**: You can also run Go code in a serverless environment using **AWS Lambda**.
- Write Go code as an AWS Lambda function and deploy it using the **AWS CLI** or **Serverless Framework**.
- **Example Deployment Command**:

```sh
Copy code
aws lambda create-function --function-name myGoFunction --runtime go1.x --handler main --zip-file fileb://function.zip
```

2. **Deploying on Google Cloud Platform (GCP)**

GCP offers several options for deploying Go applications, such as **Google Compute Engine, App Engine,** and **Cloud Run.**

- **Google Compute Engine**: Similar to AWS EC2, you can set up a virtual machine, transfer the Go binary, and run the application.

CHAPTER 16: GO IN THE CLOUD

- **Google App Engine**:
- App Engine is a fully managed platform ideal for web apps and microservices.
- **App Engine Configuration (app.yaml)**:

```yaml
Copy code
runtime: go119
entrypoint: ./myapp
```

- Deploy using:

```sh
Copy code
gcloud app deploy
```

- **Google Cloud Run**: Deploy containerized applications.
- **Steps**:

1. **Build a Docker image**:

```sh
Copy code
docker build -t gcr.io/YOUR_PROJECT_ID/myapp .
```

1. **Push to Container Registry**:

```sh
Copy code
docker push gcr.io/YOUR_PROJECT_ID/myapp
```

1. **Deploy to Cloud Run**:

```sh
Copy code
gcloud run deploy --image gcr.io/YOUR_PROJECT_ID/myapp --platform managed
```

3. **Deploying on Azure**

Azure provides services such as **Azure App Service, Azure Virtual Machines,** and **Azure Functions.**

- **Azure App Service**:
- App Service is a platform-as-a-service (PaaS) that allows you to deploy web applications quickly.
- Zip your compiled Go binary and deploy it using the Azure portal or CLI.
- **Azure Functions**:
- Azure's serverless offering supports Go functions through custom handlers.
- Use Azure's CLI to create and deploy your serverless Go functions.

Dockerizing Go Applications

Docker is a popular tool for containerizing applications, ensuring that your application and all its dependencies run consistently across different environments.

1. **Creating a Dockerfile for Go**

- **Basic Dockerfile** for Go Application:

```dockerfile
Copy code
# Stage 1: Build the Go application
FROM golang:1.19 AS builder

WORKDIR /app
COPY go.mod go.sum ./
RUN go mod download
COPY . .

RUN go build -o myapp

# Stage 2: Create a lightweight container
FROM alpine:latest

WORKDIR /root/
COPY --from=builder /app/myapp .

EXPOSE 8080
CMD ["./myapp"]
```

- **Multi-stage Builds**: The first stage builds the Go application, and the second stage creates a smaller final image.

2. **Building and Running the Docker Image**

- **Build the Docker Image**:

```sh
Copy code
docker build -t myapp .
```

- **Run the Docker Container**:

```sh
Copy code
docker run -p 8080:8080 myapp
```

3. **Benefits of Dockerizing Go Applications**

- **Portability**: Docker allows your Go application to run anywhere, regardless of the host OS.
- **Isolation**: Each container has its own environment, avoiding conflicts with other applications.
- **Scalability**: Docker containers can be easily orchestrated using tools like **Kubernetes**.

Introduction to Kubernetes and Go

Kubernetes is a container orchestration tool used to deploy, scale, and manage containerized applications. It's a natural fit for Go applications deployed in a cloud-native environment.

1. **Kubernetes Concepts**

- **Pod**: The smallest deployable unit that can run in Kubernetes, which may contain one or more containers.
- **Deployment**: Manages the desired state of Pods, including scaling and updates.
- **Service**: Exposes your Pods to the network, allowing users to access your Go application.

2. **Deploying a Go Application on Kubernetes**

To deploy a Go application, you need to create Kubernetes configuration files for **Deployments**, **Services**, and possibly **Ingress**.

- **Example Deployment (deployment.yaml)**:

```yaml
Copy code
apiVersion: apps/v1
kind: Deployment
metadata:
  name: go-app
spec:
  replicas: 3
  selector:
    matchLabels:
      app: go-app
  template:
    metadata:
      labels:
        app: go-app
    spec:
      containers:
      - name: go-app
        image: myapp:latest
        ports:
        - containerPort: 8080
```

- **Example Service (service.yaml):**

```yaml
Copy code
apiVersion: v1
kind: Service
metadata:
  name: go-app-service
spec:
  type: LoadBalancer
  selector:
    app: go-app
  ports:
```

```
      - protocol: TCP
        port: 80
        targetPort: 8080
```

3. **Deploying with kubectl**

    - **Apply the Deployment and Service:**

    ```
    sh
    Copy code
    kubectl apply -f deployment.yaml
    kubectl apply -f service.yaml
    ```

    - **Scaling the Application:**

    ```
    sh
    Copy code
    kubectl scale deployment go-app --replicas=5
    ```

4. **Benefits of Kubernetes for Go Applications**

    - **Scalability**: Kubernetes can automatically scale your Go application to handle increased traffic.
    - **High Availability**: By running multiple replicas, Kubernetes ensures that your application remains available even if individual Pods fail.
    - **Self-Healing**: If a Pod crashes, Kubernetes restarts it automatically, ensuring continuous availability.

Chapter 17: Conclusion

Congratulations on reaching the end of this book! You've covered a wide range of foundational and practical Go programming skills—from understanding Go syntax and control structures to building web applications, working with databases, and deploying your Go projects in the cloud. This concluding chapter provides direction on what to explore next to continue your Go programming journey, some advanced topics to dive into, and resources that will help you keep progressing toward Go mastery.

What's Next After This Book?

Now that you've acquired a solid understanding of Go fundamentals, it's time to take your knowledge to the next level by applying what you've learned to real-world projects, contributing to open source, and tackling more challenging aspects of Go.

1. **Building Real-World Projects**

The best way to consolidate your knowledge is by building projects. Consider:

- **Microservices**: Develop a series of microservices that interact with each other, focusing on scalability.
- **REST APIs**: Build and deploy RESTful APIs, integrating with cloud services to understand how Go works in cloud environments.
- **CLI Tools**: Go's simplicity makes it perfect for building command-line utilities. Create a tool that solves a problem you're passionate about.

2. **Contributing to Open Source**

Get involved in Go's vibrant open-source community. Contributing to projects can help you improve your skills and get feedback from experienced developers. Explore projects on GitHub, especially those written in Go, and see where you can contribute.

3. **Exploring Cloud-Native Technologies**

You've already touched upon cloud-native concepts like Docker and Kubernetes. You could expand on this by:

- Learning more about **Helm** (Kubernetes package management) and **Istio** (service mesh) to understand advanced cloud-native patterns.
- Deploying your Go applications to serverless platforms such as **AWS Lambda** or **Google Cloud Functions**.

Advanced Go Topics to Explore

As you move beyond the basics, Go has several advanced concepts and tools that can help you build more efficient and complex applications.

1. **Advanced Concurrency**

- **Worker Pools**: Learn to create worker pools that handle jobs concurrently.
- **Context Propagation**: Use the context package for managing timeouts and cancellations in concurrent applications.

2. **Reflection in Go**

Reflection allows you to inspect types and values at runtime. While often avoided in performance-sensitive code, understanding how reflection works in Go is critical when dealing with tasks such as serialization, generic handling, or working with third-party libraries.

3. **Generics**

With the introduction of **Generics** in Go 1.18, you can write more flexible and reusable code.

- Learn to write type-agnostic functions and data structures to improve the efficiency of your codebase.
- Generics can simplify data manipulation and allow you to implement common algorithms without sacrificing type safety.

4. Custom Tooling with go/* Packages

Go provides packages like go/ast, go/parser, and go/types for building custom code analysis tools.

- **Static Analysis Tools**: Develop tools that parse and analyze Go source code to identify issues, enforce standards, or optimize code.

5. Cgo: Integrating with C Libraries

Cgo allows Go to call C libraries directly. This is an advanced feature that's useful when you need to use existing C libraries or want to leverage low-level system capabilities not available in Go.

6. WebSocket and gRPC Communication

- **WebSockets**: Explore WebSockets for building real-time applications like chat apps.
- **gRPC**: gRPC allows efficient communication between services with Protocol Buffers (protobuf). It's highly performant and works well for microservices-based architectures.

7. Advanced Testing Techniques

- **Mocking and Stubbing**: Learn how to write unit tests with mocks to simulate external services.
- **Integration Testing**: Explore integration testing to verify that different parts of your system work correctly when brought together.

Resources for Continuous Learning

Continuous learning is key to staying up to date in the tech world. Below are some recommended resources to help you keep growing as a Go developer:

1. **Books**

   - **"Concurrency in Go" by Katherine Cox-Buday**: A great resource to master concurrency in Go and fully leverage goroutines.
   - **"The Go Programming Language" by Alan Donovan and Brian Kernighan**: A deep dive into Go, with exercises that will challenge and help you master the language.

2. **Online Courses**

   - **Udemy, Coursera, and Pluralsight**: These platforms offer several high-quality Go programming courses.
   - **Go.dev Learning**: The official Go site provides tutorials and guides on many advanced topics, including web development and concurrency.

3. **Online Resources and Communities**

   - **Go Blog**: The official Go blog (blog.golang.org) provides deep dives into new features, optimizations, and Go internals.
   - **Gopher Slack**: A vibrant Slack community where Go developers from around the world share tips and resources.
   - **Reddit**: Join subreddits like r/golang to discuss new developments and get advice.

4. **Frameworks and Tools**

   - Explore popular frameworks and libraries:
   - **Gin**: A fast, minimalist web framework for building APIs.
   - **GORM**: A popular ORM that provides powerful database tools.
   - **Cobra**: A library for creating CLI applications, widely used in building CLI tools with Go.

CHAPTER 17: CONCLUSION

Final Thoughts on Go Mastery

Go is an exciting and evolving programming language that shines in simplicity, concurrency, and scalability. Here are some key takeaways as you continue your journey to Go mastery:

- **Simplicity Wins**: Go was built with simplicity in mind. Avoid over-engineering solutions; stick to straightforward, maintainable code.
- **Master Concurrency**: Go's goroutines and channels are core features that make it stand out. Mastering concurrency is crucial for building high-performance, cloud-native applications.
- **Write Idiomatic Code**: Writing idiomatic Go is about more than just following conventions; it's about making your code readable, maintainable, and consistent for the Go community.
- **Stay Up-to-Date**: The Go ecosystem is constantly evolving. Generics, for example, represent a significant shift, and staying current with language features will keep you ahead of the curve.

You have now laid a solid foundation to embark on your Go programming journey. The next steps involve building more complex applications, contributing to the community, and continuously improving your skills. Remember, learning never ends—keep exploring, building, and innovating.

Good luck, and happy coding!

www.ingramcontent.com/pod-product-compliance
Lightning Source LLC
Chambersburg PA
CBHW071502220526
45472CB00003B/892